D0880830

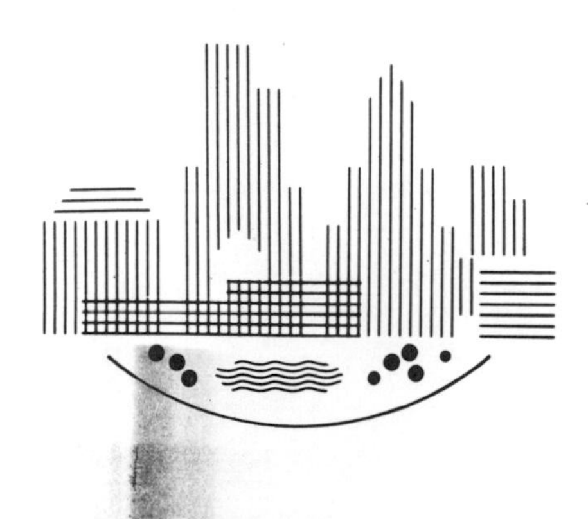

THE RISE OF URBAN AMERICA

PRINCIPLES OF CITY LAND VALUES

Richard M. Hurd

ARNO PRESS
&
The New York Times
NEW YORK • 1970

Reprint Edition 1970 by Arno Press Inc.

Reprinted from a copy in The University of Illinois Library

LC# 78-112551
ISBN 0-405-02458-4

The Rise of Urban America
ISBN for complete set 0-405-02430-4

Manufactured in the United States of America

PRINCIPLES
OF
CITY LAND VALUES

Example of highest type of improvement of short block front. A skyscraper on each corner and a low building—controlled by one or both of the skyscrapers—in the middle, giving a light well above. Broadway, between Cedar and Liberty Streets.

PRINCIPLES
OF
CITY LAND VALUES

BY

RICHARD M. HURD

President, Lawyers Mortgage Company

PUBLISHED BY

THE RECORD AND GUIDE

NEW YORK

1924

First Edition, 1903
Second Edition, 1905
Third Edition, 1911

Principles of City Land Values.

Preface.

When placed in charge of the Mortgage Department of the U. S. Mortgage & Trust Co. in 1895 the writer searched in vain, both in England and this country, for books on the science of city real estate as an aid in judging values. Finding in economic books merely brief references to city land and elsewhere only fragmentary articles, the plan arose to outline the theory of the structure of cities and to state the average scales of land values produced by different utilities within them.

The material for this study of the structure of cities—including their locations, starting points and lines of growth — has been gathered from a large number of local histories of American cities, old maps, commercial geographies, etc.

The material for the study of average scales of values has been drawn from the mass of valuations of land and buildings, rentals and mortgages, obtained in about fifty cities in the course of the mortgage business of the U. S. Mortgage & Trust Co. and also from many visits to these cities.

The viewpoint is that of a conservative lender on real estate, and, while the examples cited are chiefly from the smaller cities, it is believed that the principles stated are universal and differ only in application and in resulting combinations.

Special acknowledgment is due for aid in figuring the structural and commercial value of buildings and in the preparation of maps to Cecil C. Evers, late member of the American Institute of Architects.

Table of Contents.

Principles of City Land Values

CHAPTER I.

Introductory

THE BASIS of agricultural land values has been established since the time of Ricardo, and throws light on the fundamentals of our problem. Value in urban land, as in agricultural land, is the resultant of economic or ground rent capitalized. As first laid down, the theory of agricultural ground rents emphasized fertility as a source of rent. Later, when it was noted that it was not the most fertile lands that were first occupied but rather those nearest new settlements, accessibility or proximity to cities was recognized as an important factor in creating agricultural ground rent. In cities, economic rent is based on superiority of location only, the sole function of city land being to furnish area on which to erect buildings.

Urban economic rent is ascertained by deducting from the gross rent of land and building, first, all charges for services, such as heat, light, elevators, janitors, agents' commission for collecting rents, etc.; second, taxes, insurance, and repairs, and, finally, interest on the capital invested in the building. This interest on the cost of the building must exceed the average interest rate by an amount equal to the annual depreciation of the building, thus providing a sinking fund sufficient to replace the building at the end of its life. To make a correct showing the building must be suited to the location and managed with ordinary ability or the apparent economic rent will have little or no bearing on the value of the land.

The rate of capitalization, turning income into value, is based on the average interest rates of all investments and fluctuates with them, although within closer limits and more slowly. Wide differences occur in the rates of capitalization of rents from land of different uses in the same city, and smaller differences from land having the same use in different cities. Where a locality is advancing in value, capitalization rates are low, where stationary they are normal, and where declining they run very high. After the vital factor of prospective increase or decrease of value, the lesser factors are stability of rents, ease of convertibility,—in part by mortgaging or in whole by selling,—and character of utilization, as involving the rates of depreciation of different classes of buildings. In general, the larger the city and the higher the class of property, the greater the stability of rents, and ease of convertibility and the lower the rate of capitalization. Differences in rent are plainly apparent, but differences in rates of capitalization are frequently overlooked, although a very large proportion of value in urban land comes from a low rate of capitalization. To illustrate, of two pieces of land yielding an economic rent of $10,000 annually, one well located and improved with office building or retail shop might sell, excluding the building, on a 4 per cent. basis, or for $250,000; while the other, covered with cheap tenements, might sell, excluding the buildings, on a 10 per cent. basis, or for $100,000. The rate of capitalization is ascertained by figuring backwards, i.e., dividing average prices paid for similar land by the net income, which shows the interest rate which the community is satisfied to receive on such investments.

While intrinsic value is correctly derived by capitalizing ground rent, exchange value may differ widely from it. As ordinarily expressed, "value" means exchange value, average sales being considered the best test of value, and since all ownership lies subsequent to the date of purchase, the estimated future prospects form the mastering factor of all exchange values. Although speculation in the sense of assuming large risk for the chance of large gain is normally confined to limited sections of cities where marked changes of utility are taking place, speculation in the sense of an attempt to make money from an increase in the value of property apart from its earnings is a factor in all real estate transfers. We may note that real estate speculation is always for the rise, speculation for the fall or "short" sales being impossible, owing to the non-representative quality of land.

Even where properties are fully improved for the present use, if a new utility arises or is anticipated, since this may involve a different basis of economic rent, capitalization rate and value, by such estimated difference the exchange value may vary from the present intrinsic value. If the new utility does not arrive, prices may advance and recede, while values do not change, but if the new utility arrives, both prices and values will alter their levels.

To be reckoned with under the head of future prospects are not only local changes of utility, but the rate of growth of the city as a whole, the prosperity or depression of the surrounding section and the success or failure of the industries directly supporting it. Moreover, general financial and economic conditions enter so largely into exchange values, that values are at times not based on income, or

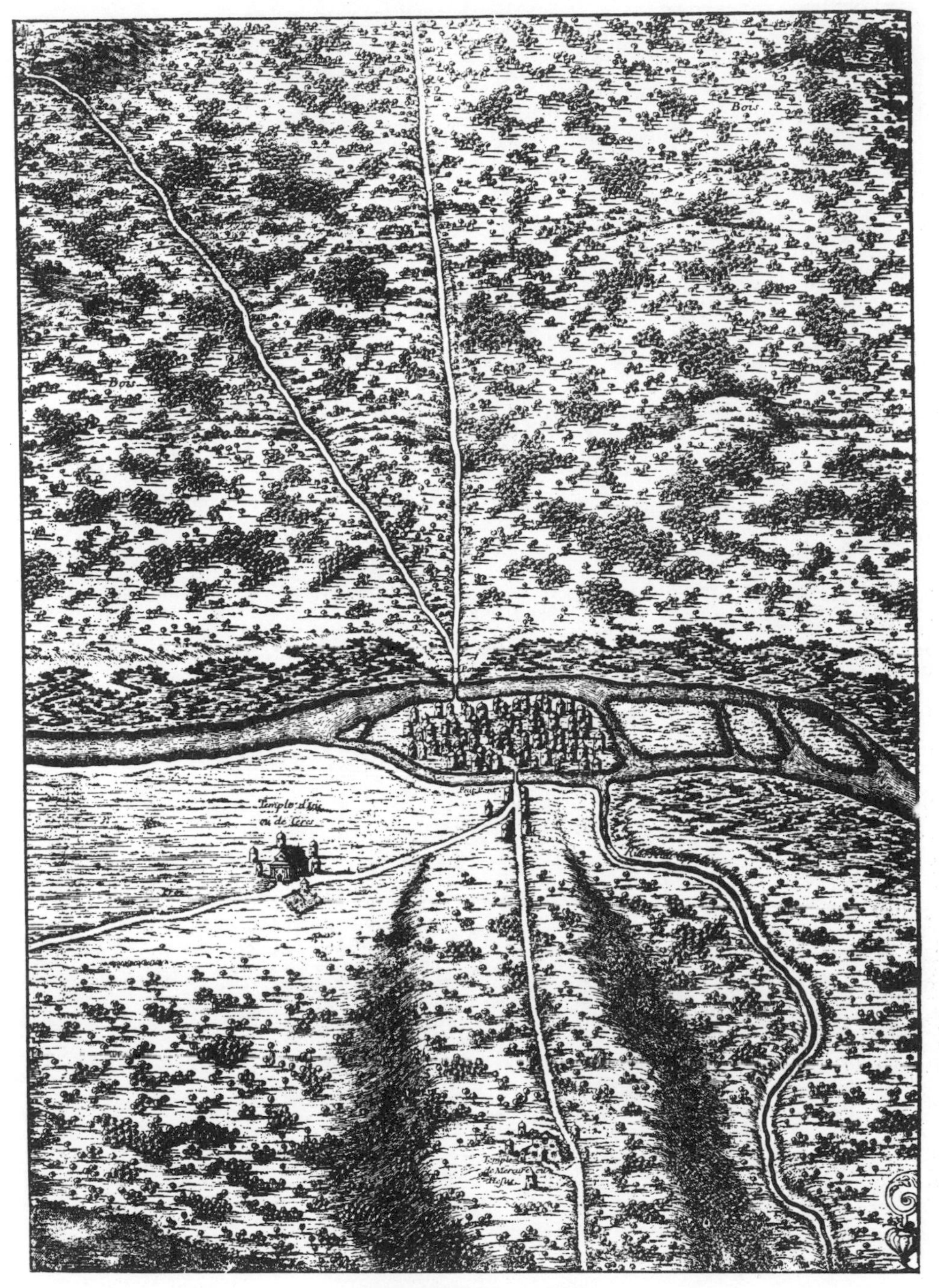

EVOLUTION OF A CITY.

Paris in 56 B. C. (Lutece) Site on Island chosen for defense. (Maps printed in 1705.)

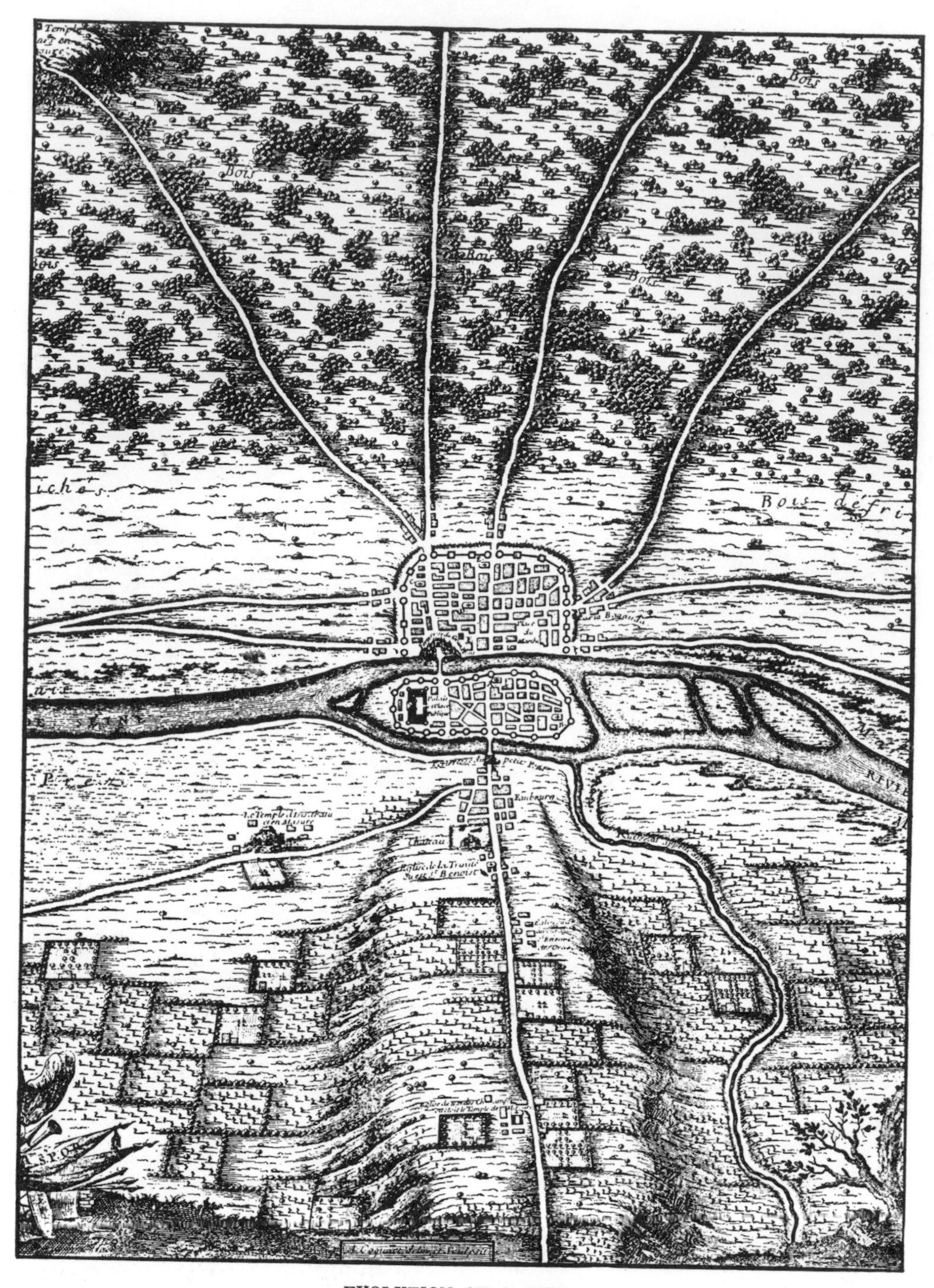

EVOLUTION OF A CITY.

Paris in 508 A. D. First walls surrounded buildings on island. Second walls on north side. First beginnings of axial growth along each road issuing from the walls.

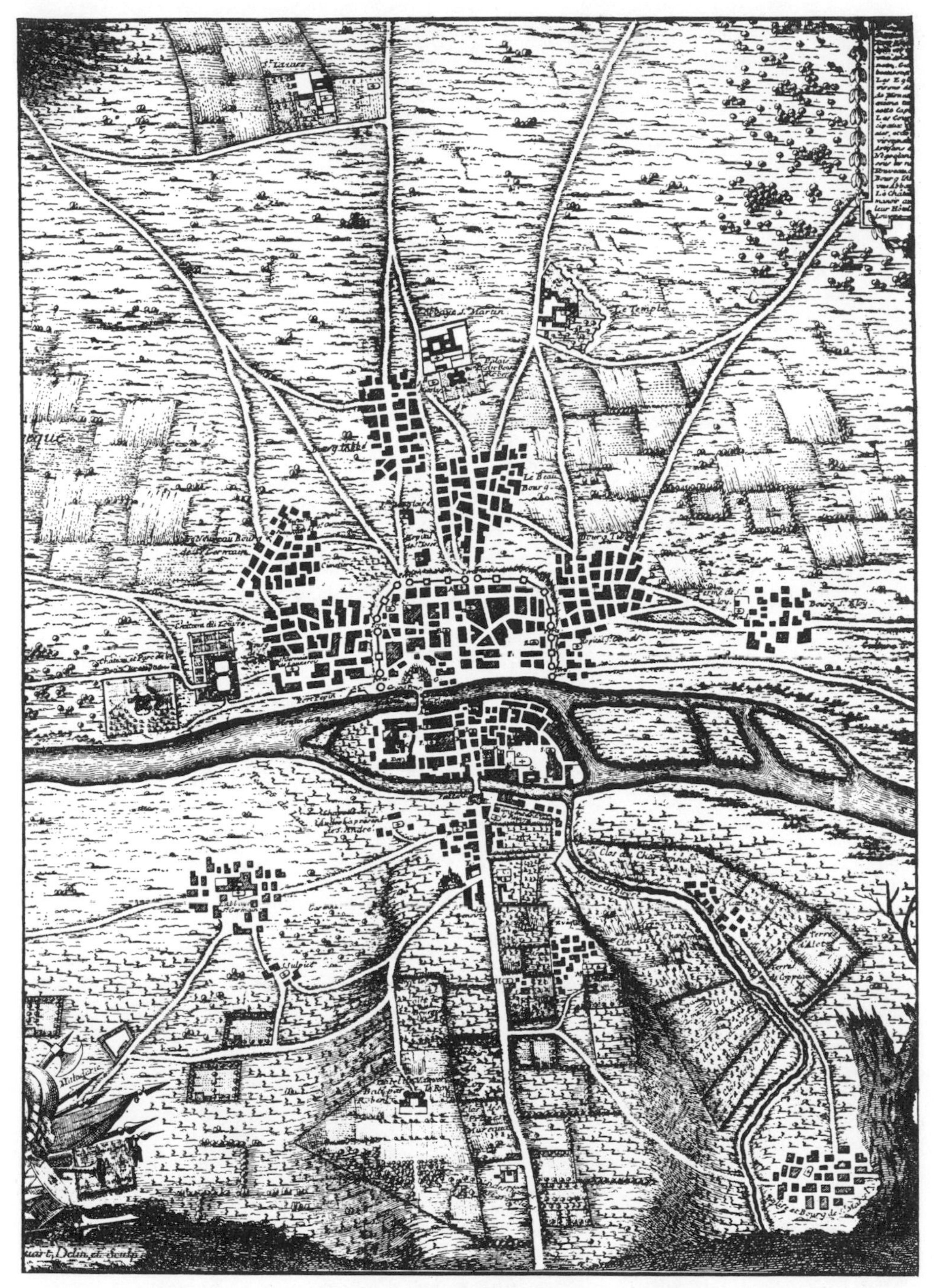

EVOLUTION OF A CITY.

Paris under Louis VII. Axial growth outside the walls has developed into centers at road intersections.

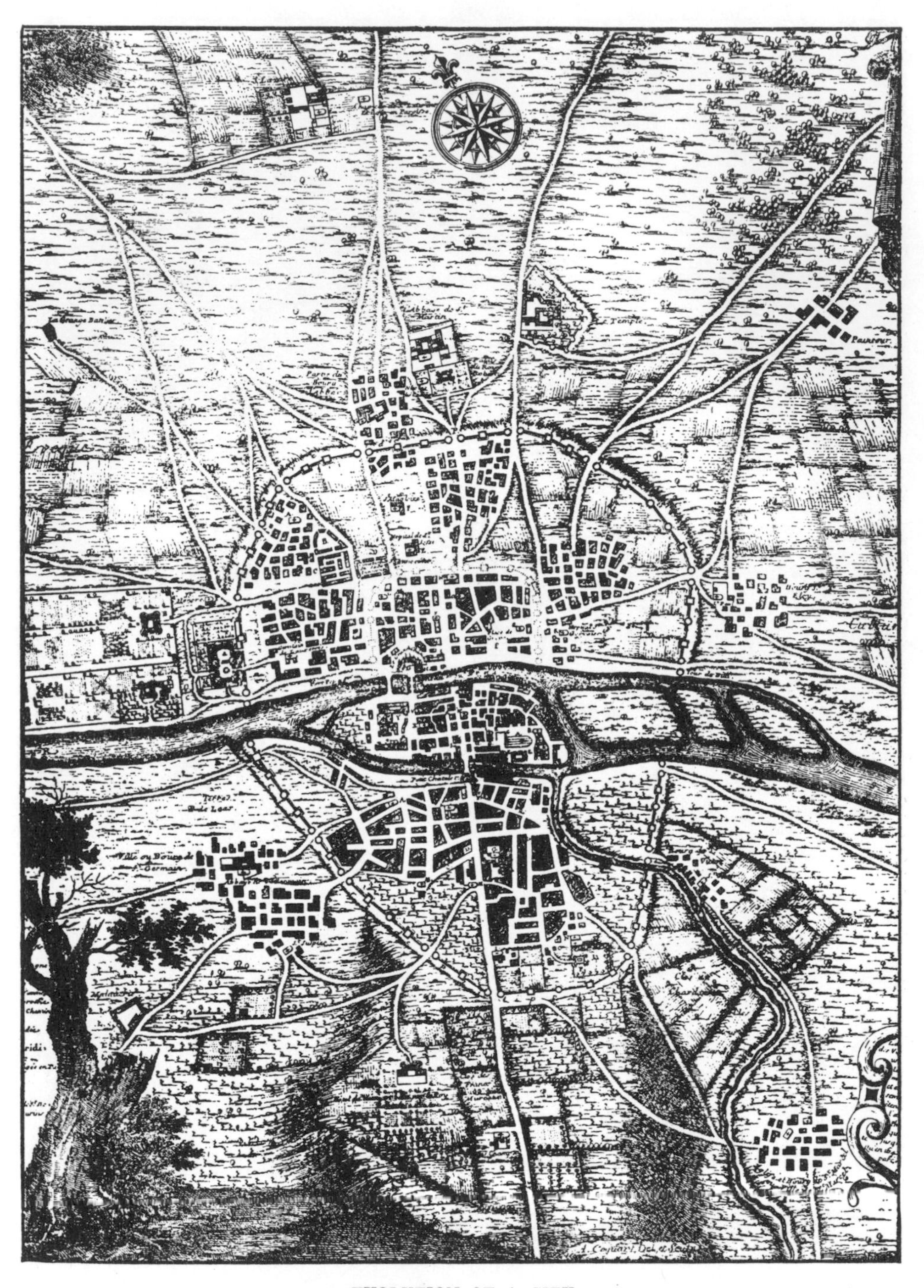

EVOLUTION OF A CITY.

Paris 1180 to 1223. New walls, include much greater area. Central growth takes place around the abbeys and churches erected mostly on the sites of the old Roman Temples.

EVOLUTION OF A CITY.

Paris 1367 to 1383. Third wall on north side includes added area. City shows marked growth on north side within the walls and on the south side, outside the walls.

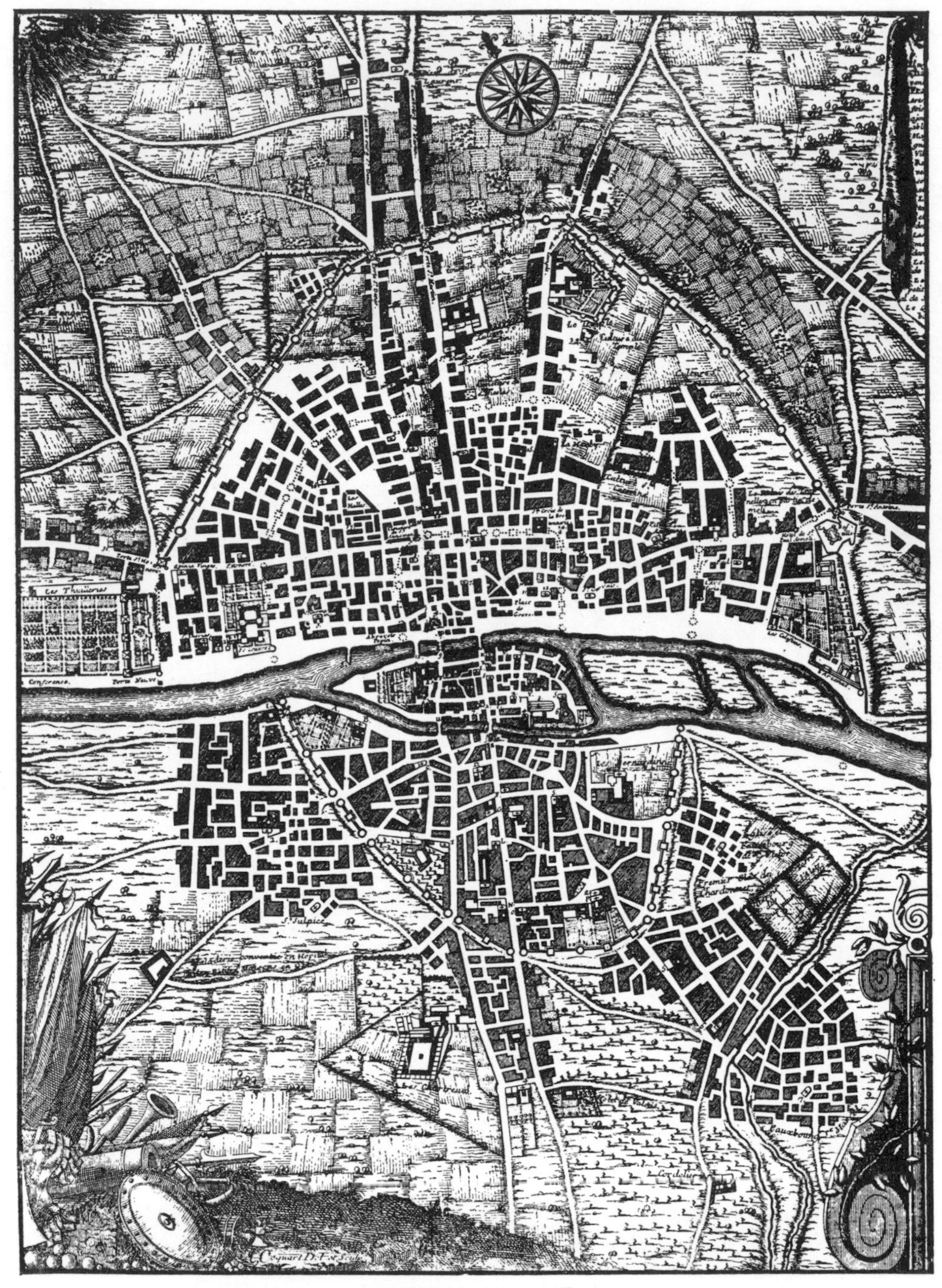

EVOLUTION OF A CITY.

Paris 1422 to 1589. The Tuilleries cause strong axial growth out the Faubourg St. Honore.

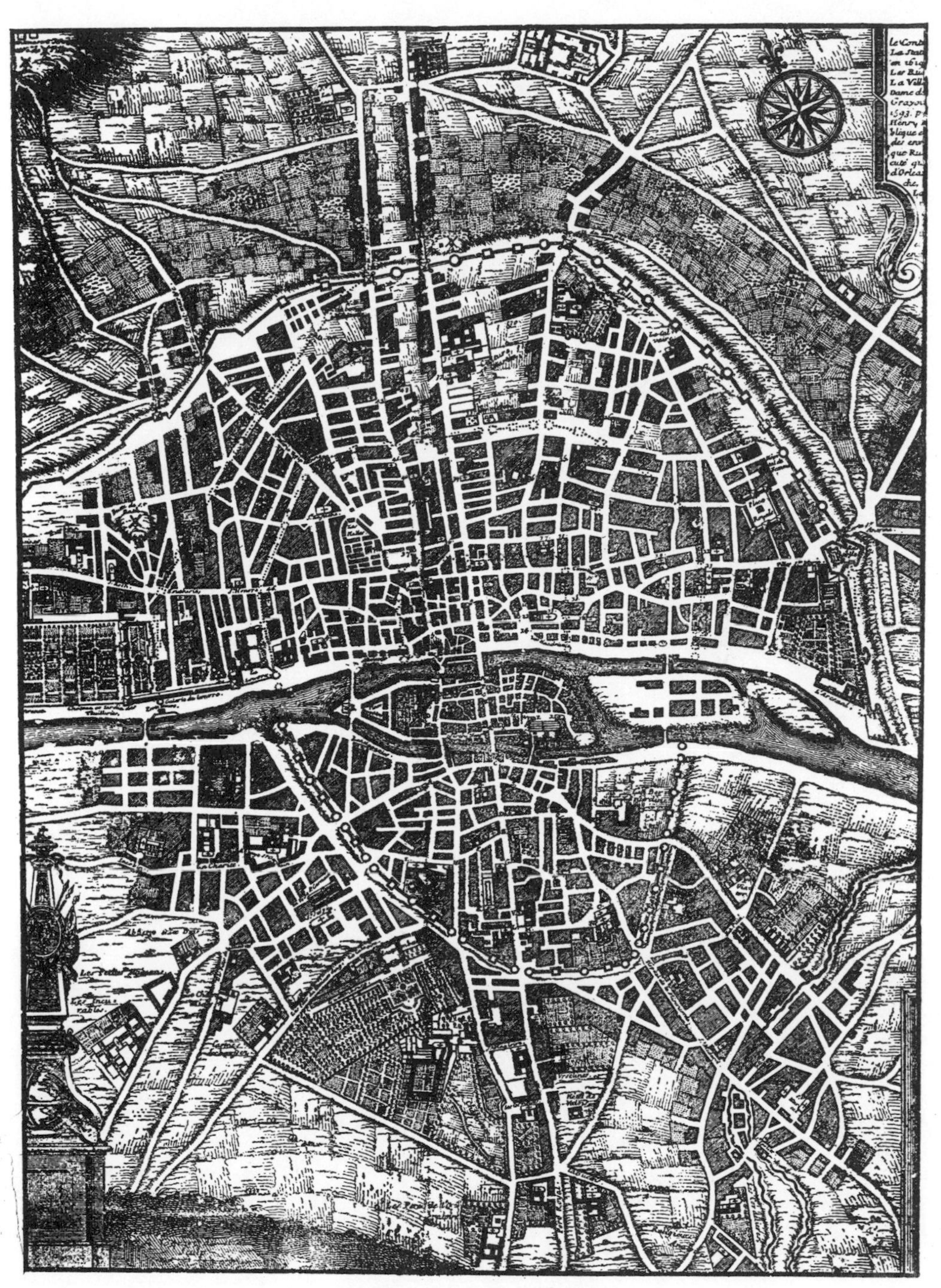

EVOLUTION OF A CITY.

Paris 1589 to 1643. The hills to the north check extension in that direction.

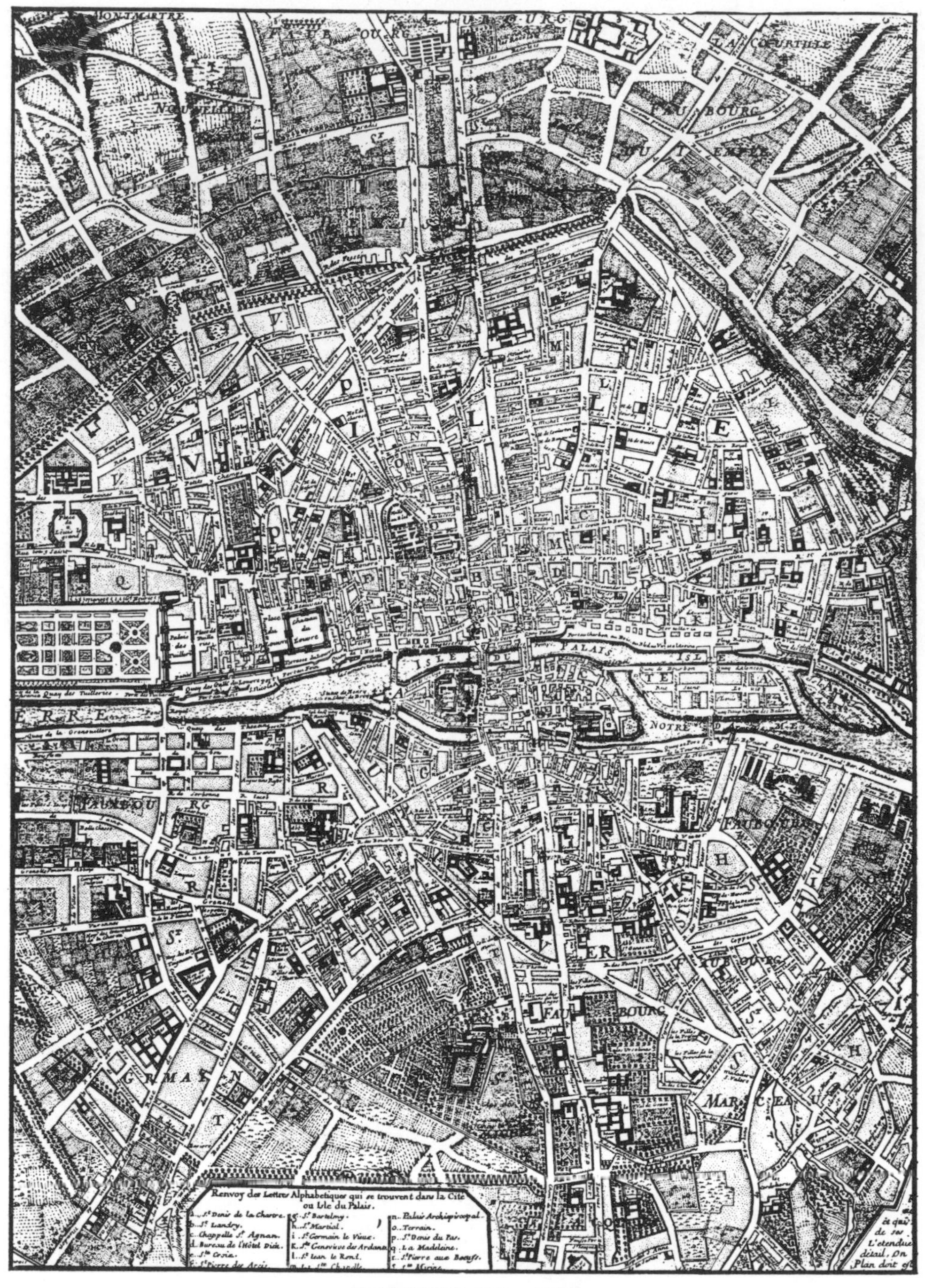

EVOLUTION OF A CITY.

Paris in 1705. The city has spread in all directions. The high land to the north is being cut up into building tracts.

supply and demand, but represent simply a condition of the public mind.

The dependence of value in land on economic rent is clearly seen in the origin of any city, utility in land arising when the first buildings are erected, but not value in land, as is evidenced by the fact that the first settlers are commonly allowed to build their houses wherever they please and enclose whatever land they need, as occurred in New York and many other cities. As a city grows, more remote and hence inferior locations must be utilized and the difference in desirability between the two grades produces economic rent in locations of the first grade, but not in those of the second. As land of a still more remote and inferior grade comes into use, ground rent is forced still higher in land of the first grade, rises

First houses in Grand Rapids, Mich. Located on river bank.

in land of the second grade, but not in the third grade, and so on. Any utility may compete for any location within a city and all land goes to the highest bidder, but owing to the limited suitability of certain areas for certain purposes, some land has but one utility. Whatever competition there is here, will be among those of the same class of utilization. Where, owing to increase or decrease of various utilizations, their area and location change, competition among different classes of utilization arises. Practically all land within a city earns some economic rent, though it may be small, the final contrast being with the city's rentless and hence, strictly speaking, valueless circumference. The prices at which land on the outskirts of a city is held may represent either the cost of platting and opening streets, or more frequently the discounting of future hopes, the chief factor lowering values being the extent of competing land due to the fact that area increases as the square of the distance from any given point.

An apparent exception to the law of no value in the site when a city starts, occurs where a city is speculatively undertaken and the lots sell at high prices in advance of utility. The difference between price and value is usually demonstrated before many years, the invariable reaction carrying the prices of lots as far below their value as they were formerly above it. Thus lots in Columbus, Ohio, which sold in 1812 at $200 to $300, sold in 1820 at $7 to $20, and more recently there are the collapses in the early history of the speculatively started towns of West Superior, Wis., Tacoma, Wash., Wichita, Kan., and Sioux City, Ia. The attempt to force economic rent into city land seems to be uniformly unsuccessful, history showing that cities grow and are not made and that human beings cannot

Ft. Wayne, 1794. Site chosen at intersection of small rivers (also of Indian trails).

be uprooted and moved in large numbers and immediately adjust themselves to the different opportunities of a new environment.

Why are ground rents paid for some locations and not for others? In general terms the difference in desirability is based on the social service which they render, or conversely, the sacrifice which they save. The land which is most convenient is first utilized, and that which is less convenient is made of service in accordance with its diminishing facilities. Since convenience means economy in time and effort, the value in any piece of land will represent the cost saved or the pleasure obtained by its use, as compared with the use of land worth nothing multiplied by the number and economic quality of the people for whom the saving is made. Thus the value of all urban land ranges from that which least serves the smallest number of people of the lowest economic quality, up to that which best serves the largest number of people of the highest economic quality.

Since value depends on economic rent, and rent on location, and location on convenience, and convenience on nearness, we may eliminate the intermediate steps and say that value depends on nearness. The next question is, nearness to what?—which brings us to the land requirements of different utilities, their distribution over the city's area and the consequent creation and distribution of values.

Our problem divides itself into two sides, one the study of the structure of cities, their origin, growth and movements; the other, an analysis of the gross rents due to various utilities, their economic rents, rates of capitalization and resulting land values.

Beginning with the structure of cities, if cities grew at random the problem of the creation, distribution and shifting of land values

Bay City, Mich., 1837. Point of origin at first dock.

would be insoluble. A cursory glance reveals similarities among cities, and further investigation demonstrates that their structural movements, complex and apparently irregular as they are, respond to definite principles. The basis of this similarity is that the same factors create all modern cities; commerce and manufactures, with political and social forces, being everywhere operative, the chief difference in influence coming from variations in their relative power.

Cities originate at their most convenient point of contact with the outer world and grow in the lines of least resistance or greatest attraction, or their resultants. The point of contact differs according to the methods of transportation, whether by water, by turnpike or by railroad. The forces of attraction and resistance include topography, the underlying material on which city builders work; external influences, projected into the city by trade routes; internal influences derived from located utilities, and finally the reactions and readjustments due to the continual harmonizing of conflicting elements. The influence of topography, all-powerful when cities start, is constantly modified by human labor, hills being cut down, waterfronts extended, and swamps, creeks and low-lands filled in, this, however, not taking place until the new building sites are worth more than the cost of filling and cutting. The measure of resistance to the city's growth is here changed from terms of land elevation or depression, and hence income cost, to terms of investment or capital cost. The most direct results of topography come from its control of transportation, the water fronts locating exchange points for water commerce, and

Marietta, Ohio, 1788. Laid out as military post with water protection on two sides.

the water grade normally determining the location of the railroads entering the city. As cities grow, external influences become constantly of less relative importance, while the original simple utilities develop into a multitude of differentiated and specialized utilities, tending constantly to segregate into definite districts.

Growth in cities consists of movement away from the point of origin in all directions, except as topographically hindered, this movement being due both to aggregation at the edges and pressure from the centre. Central growth takes place both from the heart of the city and from each subcentre of attraction, and axial growth pushes into the outlying territory by means of railroads, turnpikes and street railroads. All cities are built up from these two influences, which vary in quantity, intensity and quality, the resulting districts overlapping, interpenetrating, neutralizing and harmonizing as the pressure of the city's growth bring them in contact with each other. The fact of vital interest is that, despite confusion from the intermingling of utilities, the order of dependence of each definite district on the other is always the same. Residences are early driven to the circumference, while business remains at the centre, and as residences divide into various social grades, retail shops of corresponding grades follow them, and wholesale shops in turn follow the retailers, while institutions and various mixed utilities irregularly fill in the intermediate zone, and the banking and office section remains at the main business centre. Complicating this broad outward movement of zones, axes of traffic project shops through residence areas, create

St. Anthony, 1857, now East Minneapolis, on east side of river. Minneapolis itself originated as an overflow from St. Anthony, the starting point being determined by the bridge resting on the islands shown.

business subcentres, where they intersect, and change circular cities into star-shaped cities. Central growth, due to proximity, and axial growth, due to accessibility, are summed up in the static power of established sections and the dynamic power of their chief lines of intercommunication.

Turning to the various types of buildings occupied, we note that buildings are frequently spoken of when it is the utility carried on within them which is meant. That it is utilities and not mere buildings which are influential should be strongly emphasized, since the view is commonly held that buildings create value in land, so that where expensive buildings are erected the land will be expensive, and where cheap buildings are erected the land will be cheap. It is easy to disprove such a superficial view by noting misplaced buildings, such as a business building in a residence section, a residence in a business section, or an expensive residence or business building in the midst of cheap ones, which, even though occupied, probably do not yield enough to pay taxes. Also the buildings of an entire section may by no means evidence the value of the land, as note the handsome residences on the upper west side of New York on cheap land by contrast with the old brownstone residences on the costly land near Fifth Avenue; or witness any declining business section from which the tenants are removing, so that values are falling, although good buildings remain. Nevertheless, it is true that the quickest method of arriving at an approximate estimate of the value of land is by looking at the buildings by which it is covered, for in general buildings are properly located. To say, however, that buildings create land values is to reverse the truth,

Los Angeles in 1857. A Mexican city which has disappeared under American rebuilding.

buildings being the servants of the land and of value only as they fulfil its needs.

The continual readjustments in the life of a city, reflecting the total social relations of its inhabitants, lead to the concept of a city as a living organism. That such a concept is popularly held is shown by the common phrases, the "heart" of the city, to represent the business centre, the "arteries" of traffic to represent the streets, the "lungs" of the city to represent the parks, and, to carry the simile further, the railroad depots and wharves may be called the mouths through which the city is fed, the telephone and telegraph lines its nervous system, while man in his residence has been likened by Spencer to a particle of protoplasm surrounding itself with a cell.

One fruitful source of error in studying land values is to regard the problem as involving only a point of time instead of a period of time. Any violation based on present facts alone is incomplete, consideration of past influences and future prospects being vitally necessary. The life of value in land, whether the unit taken is a city, a section of a city, or a single lot, bears a close analogy to all other life in being normally characterized by a small beginning, gradual growth and increased strength, up to a point of maximum power, after the attainment of which comes a longer or shorter decline to a final disappearance. Thus all value in city land undergoes a con-

Chattanooga, 1863. Population chiefly soldiers. Market Street from 5th to 8th Streets, shown in center of picture (even then the principal street).

tinuous evolution from a state of non-existence through a cycle of changes, to a final dissolution, or to a new birth, when the process is repeated on the same land. One more qualification should be made limiting the working of economic laws, viz., the individual factor, which may create or destroy cities, sections within cities, or individual properties within sections. A striking uniformity exists, however, in the obedience of individuals to economic laws, self-interest being a compelling factor so that individual sections, especially on the negative or destructive side, may be classed as exceptions.

Underneath all economic laws, the final basis of human action is psychological, so that the last stage of analysis of the problems of the structure of cities, the distribution of utilities, the earnings of the buildings which house them, and the land values resulting therefrom, turn on individual and collective taste and preference, as shown in social habits and customs.

CHAPTER II.

Forces Creating Cities

DEFENSE AGAINST enemies, the chief factor in primitive times creating cities, survived as an influence affecting the first settlements in this country, the early forts on the Atlantic Coast and in the West drawing population around them in the same way that the Roman camps on the borders of the Danube and Rhine, and the Cossack camps in southern Russia started cities. With the establishment of civilized government the necessity for defence has vanished and population is concentrated either by commerce or manufactures, or by the less important political and social factors.

Commerce, or the distribution of commodities, involves their storage and transfer, and requires warehouses, docks and freight depots, while the population engaged in this business requires residences, shops and public buildings. Where the products handled are of low value, and the handling is a simple trans-shipment, the result of even a large flow of commodities in locating population at a point of trans-shipment may be small. It is when the transfer of goods is accompanied by a breaking of bulk or by a change of ownership, there being then added the complex mechanism of commercial exchange performed by importers, exporters, wholesalers, retailers, insurers, brokers and bankers, that wealth' is accumulated and localized, with consequent power to control business for local benefit.

Manufactures are of constantly increasing importance in city growth, owing to the development of the factory system and the advantages of labor supply, transportation, and markets in the larger cities. Diversified manufactures are a creation of the last fifty years, the law of development being an evolution from a rough working of coarser forms of necessary articles in the newer sections of a country, through various grades of refining and specialization, to a great variety of necessaries and luxuries in the older and more populous sections. A city created solely by manufactures is a modern development, among such being Essen, Germany; Pullman, Ill., and South Bend, Ind.

Political forces operate to build up a city when it is the seat of national, state or county government, either legislative, executive or judicial, or all combined. The administration of government as a single factor has created but few cities, Alexandria furnishing an ancient example, St. Petersburg, Moscow and Washington later examples, and in this country a few state capitals being arbitrarily started, such as Columbus, O., Indianapolis, Ind., and Lincoln, Neb. Nevertheless the rapid growth of Berlin, London and Vienna has been largely due to the centralizing of national government in those cities. In many American state capitals, city growth is injured by public attention being diverted from business to politics.

Boston Back Bay about 1845. Since filled in and made the most fashionable residence section of the city.

All other factors creating cities may be broadly classed as social, cities being centres of culture and furnishing education, art, fashion, intellectual stimulus and amusements to their tributary country. The social factor operates in direct ratio to the size of the city, social ambition and opportunities constituting a steady attracting force through the various grades of cities, migration being from the farm to the village, from the village to the town and from the town to the city. Thus the fact that New York counts among its inhabitants the great majority of American millionaires is of vital importance in maintaining its luxurious standard of hotels, shops, theatres, clubs and restaurants, which in turn attract the pleasure-seeking travel of this country. In so far as a city is a market or consuming centre, business is created and population attracted, cities in some cases being consuming points only, such as Atlantic City, St. Augustine, Newport, etc., where wealth is not created, but a city is required to minister to those distributing wealth.

All cities which have attained any considerable size include in varying proportions all the above factors of commerce, manufactures, political and social forces. In each city the sections built up by the different factors may be clearly distinguished, these flourishing or decaying according to the prosperity or decline of their special factors. Thus the railroads, docks and warehouses evidence the city's commerce; the factories its industrial energies; the retail shops the consuming power of the population; the residence sections the wealth, social grades and numbers of the citizens; and the buildings of public and semi-public utility the standard of civilization and civic pride of the city.

The underlying factors which start all the processes creating and distributing wealth are the energy and enterprise of the people, these being in the last analysis the sole sources of wealth. Raw materials, waterways, favorable climate and other natural advantages are only indirectly decisive and always presuppose men to exploit them.

CHAPTER III.

Location of Cities

SITUATIONS FAVORABLE for defence determined the location of ancient cities, as with the Greek colonies on a promontory or an island, the Etruscan cities on hill tops, Athens with the Acropolis, Rome on seven hills, Paris on an island and London in the midst of swamps. In modern times the individual settler locates his cottage to satisfy his first needs for water, wood, grass, shelter, etc., and small settlements are widely scattered in all available spots. It is largely geographical superiority which renders certain localities capable of satisfying more extensive demands and lifts small settlements into cities.

Trade routes, the lines of least resistance between the sources of products and their final markets, have in all ages located commercial cities at the points where a break in transportation occurs. Where a trade route traverses an ocean or lake, cities arise at the harbors which have easy topographical approach from productive regions and from which markets can be readily reached. For example, the phenomenal growth of New York is due to there being but one topographically easy route from the West through the Appalachian Range to the Atlantic Coast, concentrating the flow of products to New York, aided first by the Erie Canal and later by the New York Central and other railroads. Where a gulf exists, the trading city is commonly located at the innermost angle, as with Christiana, Liverpool, Genoa, Naples, Venice and Hamburg. Where the action of the sea closes harbors, ancient cities were ruined, as with Ephesus, Utica, and the coast cities of Asia Minor and northern Africa, while modern cities retain their harbors by constant dredging.

Where the trade route follows a river, cities arise either near the mouth where ocean and river navigation meet, as at New Orleans or Philadelphia; at the head of rivers where river and creek navigation meet, as at Albany, Richmond and St Paul; at the confluence of two or more rivers or branches of the same river, as at St. Louis, Omaha, Mayence, Coblentz, and Cairo; at the intersection of a river and a canal, as at Richmond, Syracuse, Evansville, and Fort Wayne; at an obstruction in the river requiring unloading, as formerly at

Louisville, or at a marked bend changing the direction of a river, as at Cincinnati, Kansas City, Madgeburg, Toulouse, and Lyons.

A river in forming a natural highway forms also a natural barrier to intercourse between its two sides, so that facilities for crossing the river may so concentrate travel as to create a small trade route and thus a town at the river crossing. For example, Harrisburg started at a ferry across the Susquehana River; Rockford

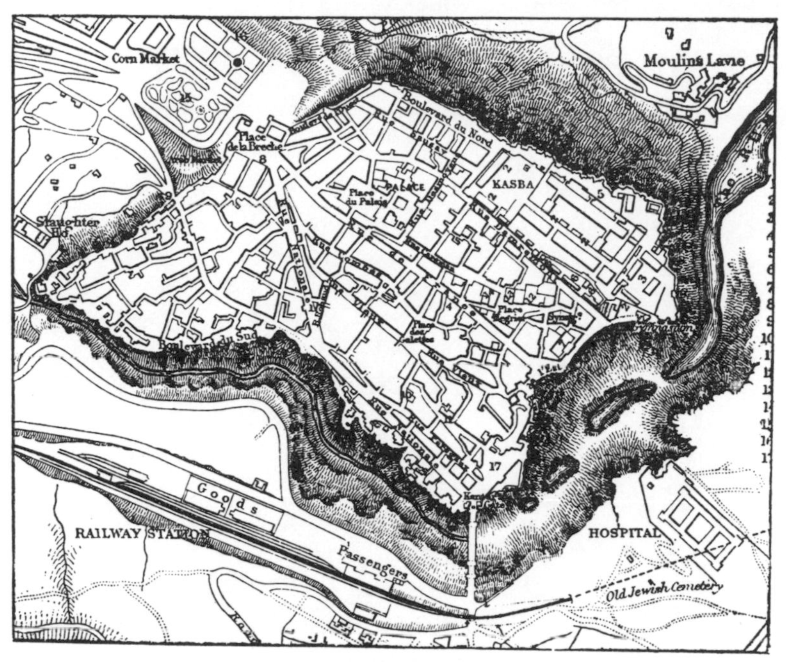

Constantine, North Africa. Typical site of ancient Mediterranean city on flat-topped hill, chosen for defence.

and Reading at fords in the Rock and Schuylkill Rivers, and Terre Haute at the bridge of the National Pike across the Wabash River. Deep water in rivers will locate cities, as with Memphis, Vicksburg, Natchez, Bremen, Rotterdam, Antwerp, and Havre. New Orleans owes its location to the fact that the land on which it was built was a few feet higher than any river land within many miles of it.

Land trade routes, prior to the time of railroads, created cities at their intersections, commonly in the centre of great plains, as with Paris, Vienna, Moscow, Berlin, and Prague. Other points were where plain and mountain met, requiring a change in transportation, as with Turin, Milan, Augsburg and Munich. The old trails from the Missouri River to the West caused the beginning of a number of towns as outfitting points, such as Council Bluffs, St. Joseph and Topeka.

When railroads were invented, they superseded all other land trade routes, and owing to the greater economy, both in the construction and operation of railroads which follow a water grade, their influence has in most cases strengthened existing cities located by water routes. The exceptions to this occur where railroads run

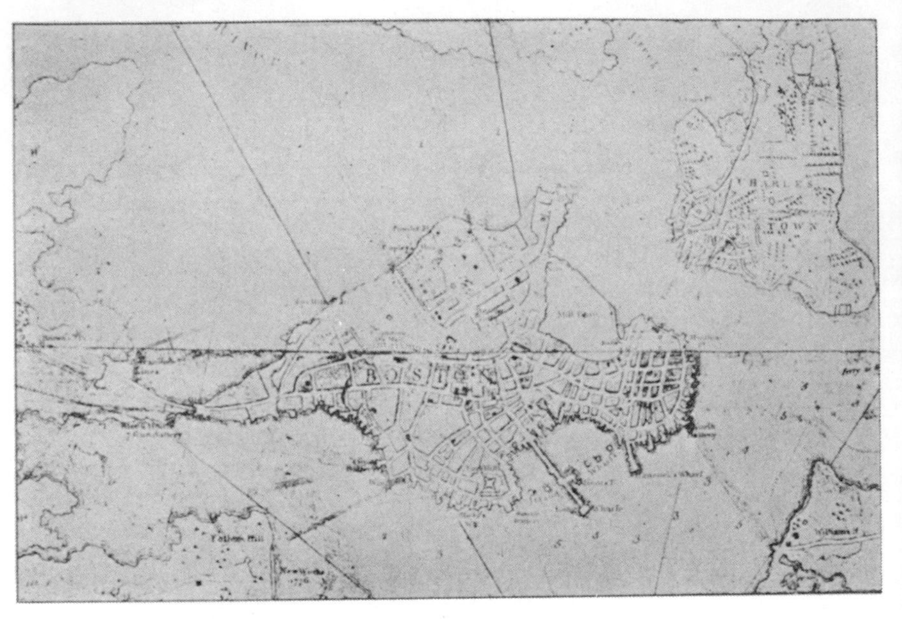

Boston, 1777, showing how nearly the site was an island; site chosen chiefly for protection against Indians and wolves.

contrary to the general topography of the country, as in the Mississippi Valley, the trade routes now running east and west and not, as originally anticipated, north and south; where mountain barriers are overcome by means of tunnels, such as those under the Alps and the Cascades, and where railroads in process of building have made temporary terminal points, which started cities, as with Worcester and Atlanta.

In manufacturing, the extractive industries locate near raw materials, lumber mills being built near forests, as in Saginaw, Bay City, Minneapolis, and Seattle; iron foundries near iron or coal mines, as in Pittsburgh; smelters near gold and silver mines, as in

Denver and San Francisco; salt works near salt wells, as in Syracuse, and formerly in Lincoln; oil refineries near oil wells, as in Cleveland; salmon canneries near the waters where salmon run, as in Portland and Seattle; fruit canneries near orchards, as in Los Angeles and San José; beet sugar factories in or near beet sugar fields, as in Saginaw and Bay City. The extractive industries migrate as raw materials are exhausted. Thus the lumber industry has moved from Maine to Michigan, Wisconsin, Minnesota, and finally

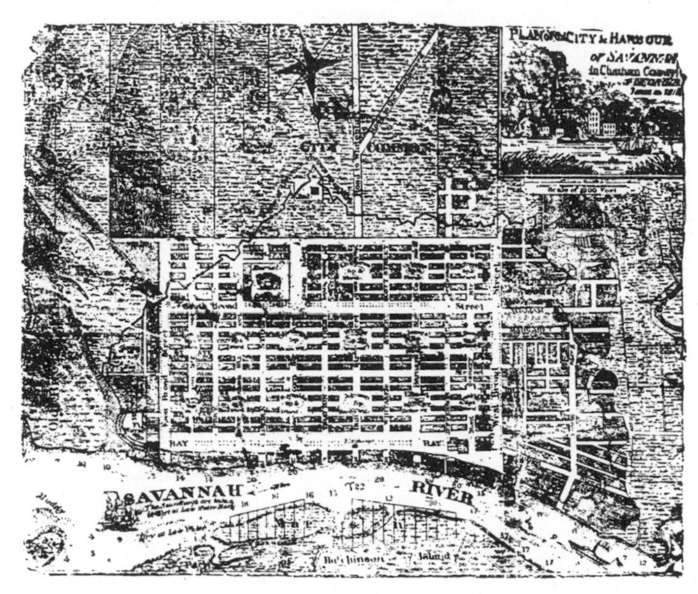

Savannah, 1818. Showing line of fortifications, also rice swamps on either side, which have restrained growth of city to one direction.

the Pacific Coast, and the meat-packing industry from New York to Buffalo, Indianapolis, Chicago, and finally Kansas City, Omaha, and St. Joseph, near the centre of the corn belt.

Water power, when of sufficient volume and fall and located in a section of natural resources, has created many cities, such as Fall River, Lowell, Minneapolis, Spokane, and Schaffhausen. Also in many cities water power greatly stimulated the early growth, although steam has since supplanted it, as in Providence and Philadelphia. The recent development of electric transmission of water power for long distances is promoting the growth of Buffalo, Los Angeles, Salt Lake City, Portland, Ore., and Seattle.

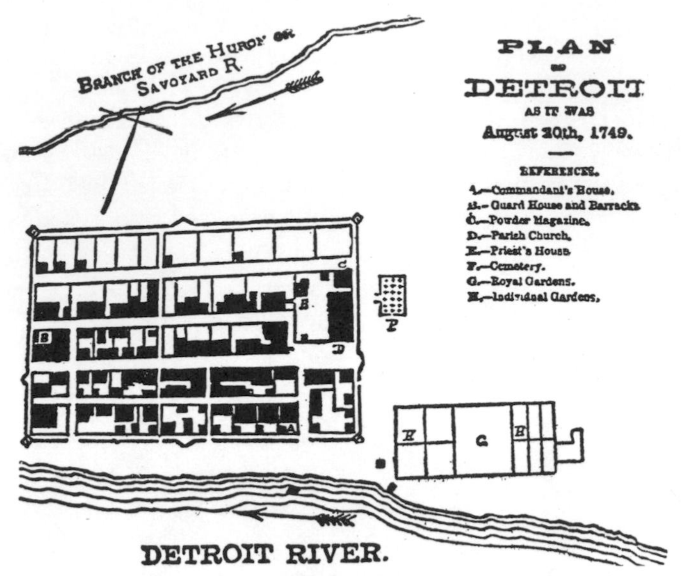

Detroit, 1749. Showing old plat and first houses within the fortifications.

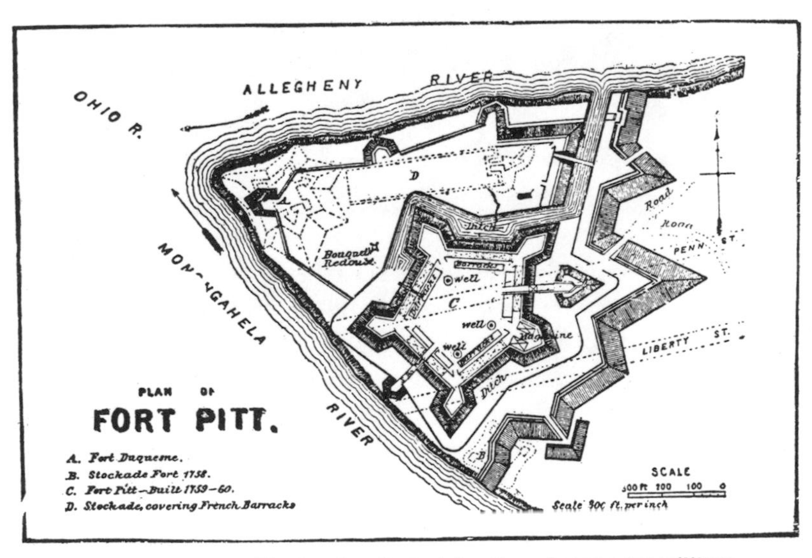

Starting point of Pittsburgh. Fort at junction of rivers for military reasons.

As industries become more specialized a steady supply of highly trained labor becomes of greater importance, tending to draw them to the larger cities, but opposed to this is the greater danger of strikes in large cities, which creates a slight counter movement towards smaller villages. A further argument for the larger cities is that they furnish a home market for much of the product, and that being located on trade routes low transportation rates are given, the commercial and industrial factors thus reacting on each other. Climate is a factor to be reckoned with in the textile industries, cotton and woolen manufactures being aided by a moist atmosphere. The general tendency of manufacturing seems to be, first, to create many small towns, and later to promote the growth of the larger cities already started by commerce.

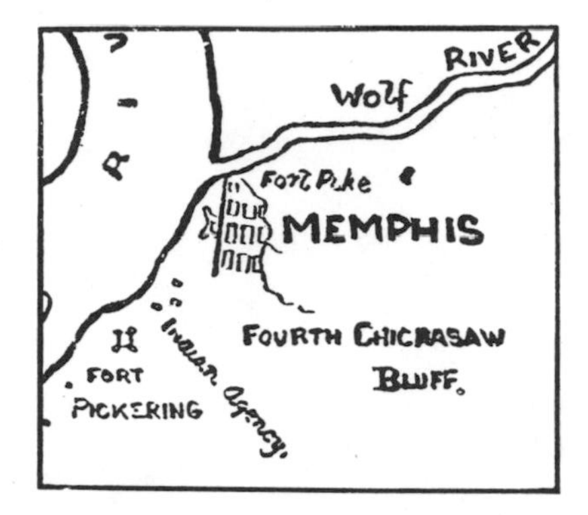

First map of Memphis, showing start of city at junction of Wolf River and Mississippi River.

Where politics govern in selecting a city site the location is ordinarily a compromise. Thus Washington was located half way between the north and the south, before the west was developed, and Columbus and Indianapolis were located at the geographical centres of their respective states. The influence of climate in locating cities is shown in such summer resorts as Newport, Bar Harbor, and Lenox, and such winter resorts as Los Angeles, St. Augustine, Atlantic City, and Pasadena.

The exact starting point of cities is worth noting, since all growth consists of movement away from it. To say that a city owes its location to a harbor, to the head of river navigation or to a fertile inland plain, is somewhat indefinite, since a large part of the harbor may be neglected and valueless, and the head of river navigation and the inland plain may furnish many other locations apparently equally desirable and yet not utilized. In the early days when protection was all-important, the fort was the point of origin, but with commercial cities the starting point is the most convenient point of contact with the outer world; this being a wharf where deep water and a high bank meet, if transportation is by water, the intersection of turnpikes topographically located, if transportation is by wagon, and a railroad depot placed for the convenient shipping of products, if transportation is by rail. With river cities the require-

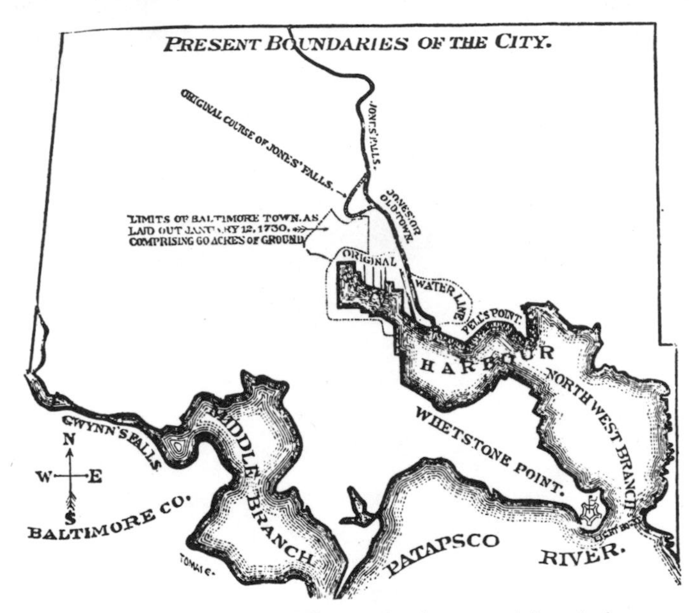

Baltimore as laid out, 1730, and showing present boundaries.

ment of deep water and a high bank, and further, the avoidance of swift currents, was frequently best met where a creek ran into a river, the first docks of New York being on the creek where Broad Street now is; of Philadelphia, where Dock Creek joined the Delaware River; of Toledo, where Swan Creek joined the Maumee River; of Memphis, where Wolf Creek joined the Mississippi River, and of Richmond, where Shockoe's Creek joined the James River. Where steep hills descend close to the water's edge there are in some instances two starting points for the town, one for business buildings at the water's edge and the other for residences on the hill, as at Richmond, Knoxville, and Kansas City. At Omaha, owing to variations in the height of water, the town started about ten blocks back from the waterfront.

Where the first settlers, having in mind a future city, lay out a plat at the inception of the city, the starting point of the city may be determined arbitrarily, the central point being a public square or a public building. Corporate or private ownership is in some cases sufficiently powerful to alter the location of a city, either by forcing it away from the original point of the older settlement, as at West Superior and Tacoma, or by preventing it from occupying its normal site, as at Houston.

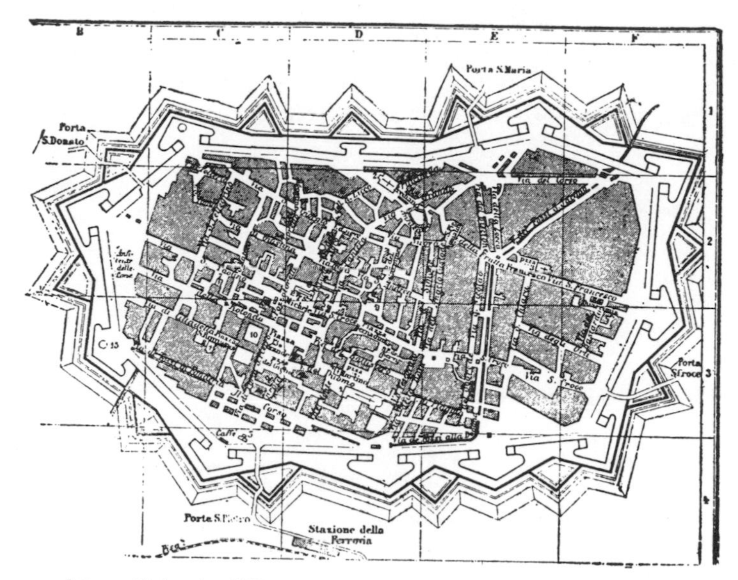

Lucca, Italy, in 1870. Example of European city surrounded by fortifications, tending to concentrated land utilization.

Sometimes the first location of a city is so unsatisfactory that the entire settlement is moved, as with Akron, O., where the soil did not hold the water from the power canal for the flour mill. Hence the mill was moved and the town followed. Also Charleston, S. C., first started on the west bank of the Ashley River, and Mobile moved in 1710 from 27 Mile Bluff. Small towns have been bodily moved either to avoid municipal debt or to secure better locations. Recently in the Dakotas several towns were moved on rollers from six to twelve miles, from the small rivers on which they were first built to the new extension of the Chicago, Burlington & Quincy R. R. In most cases vested interests, both in the buildings and in the value of the land, are too powerful to permit of a wholesale moving, the efforts of inhabitants being aimed towards counteracting any deficiencies of location by increased or differently directed labor.

While we may properly speak of cities as having started from one centre, the largest cities have swallowed up many villages and towns, both their own offshoots and independent settlements. Thus New York absorbed Greenwich, Chelsea, Bowery, Harlem, Brooklyn, Long Island City, etc.; Philadelphia absorbed Spring

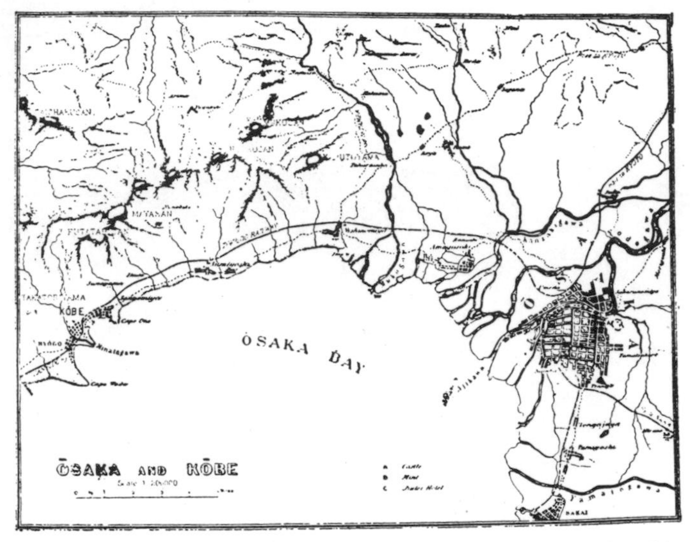

Osaka and Kobe, Japan Example of city, back from waterfront with smaller city serving as a port.

Garden, Northern Liberties, Kensington, Southwalk, Moyamensing, etc., and Boston absorbed Roxbury, Dorchester, Charleston, Brighton, East Boston, South Boston, etc. The impetus of the chief city is so great as to practically obliterate the influence of the smaller towns.

The importance of studying the geographical location of cities is due to the insight thus obtained into their structure, the distribution of population conforming to the same principles within a city as without. Topography operates in a similar manner, whether within or without a city, in causing population to flow along the same levels. Water surfaces, whether within or without a city, if navigable, facilitate the movement of population, and if non-navigable prevent it. The law of continuity is the same, every city being a link

Ancient Alexandria. Rectangular plat laid out by the Royal architect.

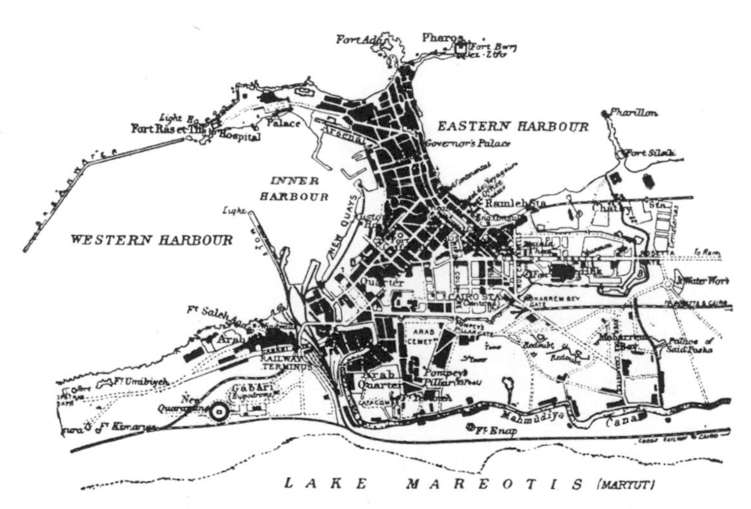

Modern Alexandria. City shifted onto the former Island of Pharos
Reversion to irregular plattings.

in the chain stretching from the first settlements in a country to the last, and every growth within a city a part of the chain of development which first reaches the city from the outside and continues its life within. Manufacturing has the same centralizing effect, whether on a large scale it creates a city or on a small scale it builds up a district within a city. The small streams of products from the farm, the forest or the mine flowing together on the way to their markets, create trade routes, and similarly the inhabitants of a city, controlled by economic forces and flowing together on their daily way to their places of business, create traffic streets or city trade routes. Railroads which create cities at their terminals and, in lesser degree, at their transfer points, have their counterpart in street railroads which draw utilities and values to their terminals, and, in lesser degree, to their lines and street intersections. Finally, the law of gravitation, which draws bodies together in direct proportion to their mass and in inverse proportion to their distance, operates similarly in drawing together two cities or in drawing together two sections within the same city.

CHAPTER IV.

Ground Plan of Cities

THE FIRST step in studying the ground plan of cities is to note the topographical faults which normally control the shape of cities, by interfering with their free growth in all directions from their points of origin. These are of two kinds: water surfaces, such as harbors, lakes, rivers, creeks and swamps, or sharp variations from the normal city level, such as steep hills, deep hollows and ravines.

Water surfaces may either leave islands on which a city originates, as with New York and Galveston; promontories at the mouths of rivers, as with Boston and Portland, Me.; promontories between two rivers, as with Philadelphia and Pittsburgh, or may consist of lakes scattered through the city's site, as with Minneapolis, Seattle and Grand Rapids; of rivers, as at Fort Wayne and Dayton; creeks, as at New Haven and Toledo; or marshes, as at New Orleans and Savannah. The rivers may have either a straight front, as at Albany, St. Paul and Portland, Ore.; a curved front leaving a convex site, as at Cincinnati, Louisville and Memphis, or may be combined with small rivers and creeks, intersecting the city's site in various ways. The deep harbors, lakes and rivers cannot be filled in, so that, as far as they extend, they furnish an outline for the city. Increasing demand for land, however, may project growth across the deep water surfaces and form suburban settlements beyond them. The power of rivers to hold growth on the side where the city originates depends on their width, on the area and relative advantages of the sites on the two sides of the river, and on speculative enterprise. At St. Louis, New Orleans and Kansas City, where the river is wide and the land across the river not attractive, the river forms practically an absolute bar to growth. At Toledo, Portland, Ore., Cincinnati, Pittsburgh and Des Moines, many bridges connect the two sides and minimize the deterring effect of the river.

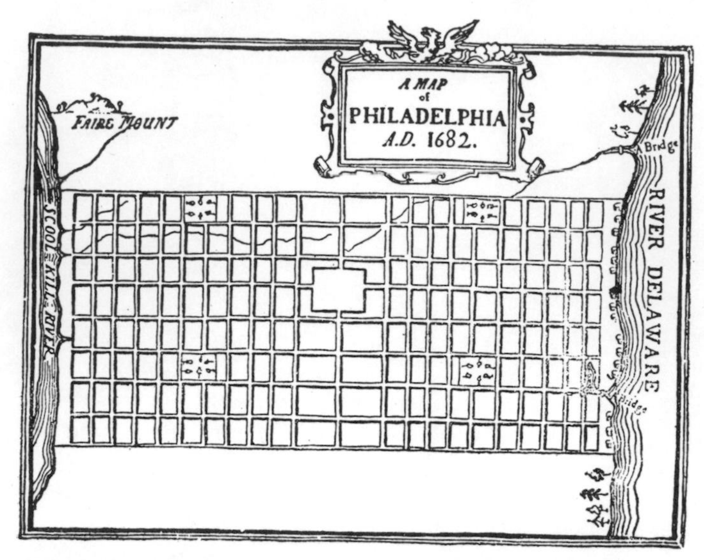

Philadelphia, 1682. Old plat shows central square, now the municipal center.

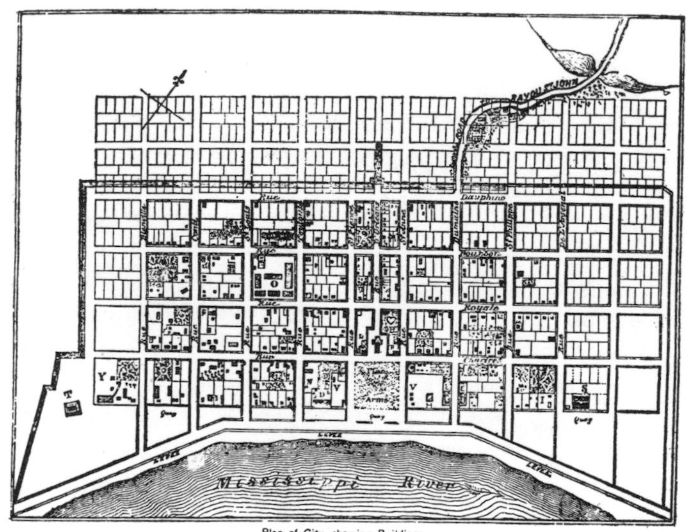

Plan of City, showing Buildings.

New Orleans, about 1728. Old French city; canal on the west later became Canal St., and American city built west of it.

Creeks are of chief importance when their erosion has worn a deep and wide ravine, the difference in level constituting a bar to a city's growth rather than the creek itself. When the creek is narrow it is frequently covered over and ceases to exert any influence, as in New York, Richmond, and other cities.

Swamps limit growth, for example preventing Philadelphia from growing south, and Savannah from growing east and west. On the other hand, New Orleans is largely built on a swamp, important

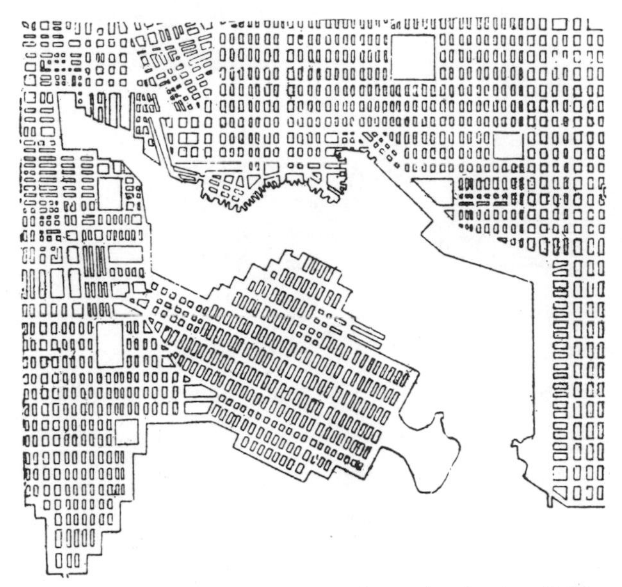

Example of platting parallel to irregular water fronts. Baltimore.

parts of Washington and Syracuse were formerly swamps, and in the lower part of New York the Collect Pond, Lispenard Meadows, Beekman Swamp, etc., have been filled in and obliterated.

After a city has spread over the original levels and climbed some moderate elevations, the demand for land may cause a filling in of the lower levels. In Boston the Back Bay district was created by filling; in Chicago, after the great fire of 1871, the city was raised from seven to ten feet; in San Francisco from Montgomery Street east was formerly mud flats; and the process of filling in land for business purposes continually goes on in the majority of water front cities.

The influence of topography may be summarized by saying that level land attracts business, moderate elevations attract residences, land below the normal level attracts transportation lines, and filled-in land is generally used for warehousing, manufacturing and cheap tenements.

The main direction of city growth is usually controlled by topography. For example, the cities at the west end of harbors or on the west side of rivers grow west, as Boston, San Francisco, St. Louis, Omaha, Minneapolis; cities on the east side of harbors or rivers grow east, as Columbus, St. Joseph, Memphis, Grand Rapids, Seattle, and similarly New York, Philadelphia, Detroit, New Orleans, Milwaukee, Indianapolis grow north; and Louisville, Kansas City, Savannah, Houston grow south. The impression that the points

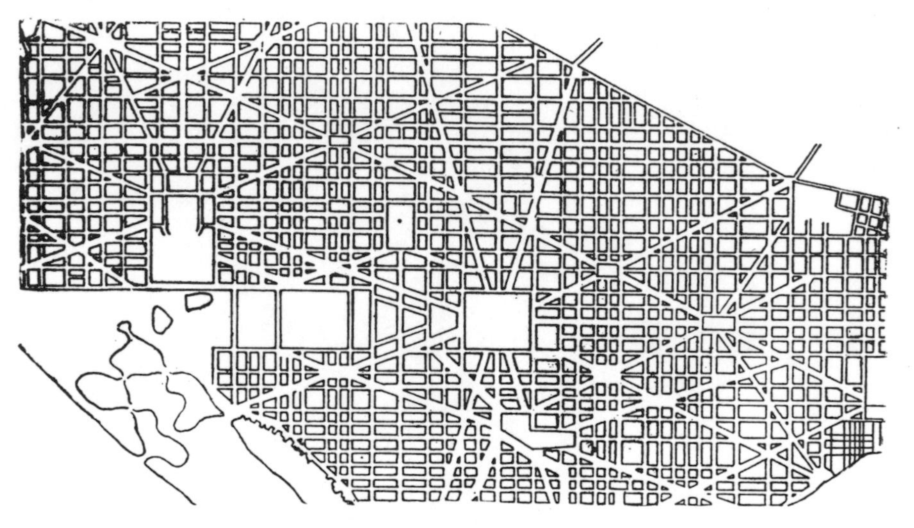

Example of diagonal avenues superimposed on rectanglar platting. Washington.

of a compass affect the direction of city growth is based on the statement that the majority of English and German cities are growing west, owing to the prevailing west winds which drive away the dense smoke from soft coal and render the west end of these cities the preferable residence sections. No such general tendency, however, exists in this country.

As to their laying out, cities may be divided into two classes, those which have grown up without any definite plan and those whose ground plan has been laid out in advance of growth. The cities which have grown up haphazard exhibit a tangle of narrow and crooked streets of varying and irregular size, evolved from cow paths or old trails, whose directions were originally influenced by trifling obstacles, such as hillocks, rocks or clumps of trees. These first streets left large tracts between them, which were later pierced

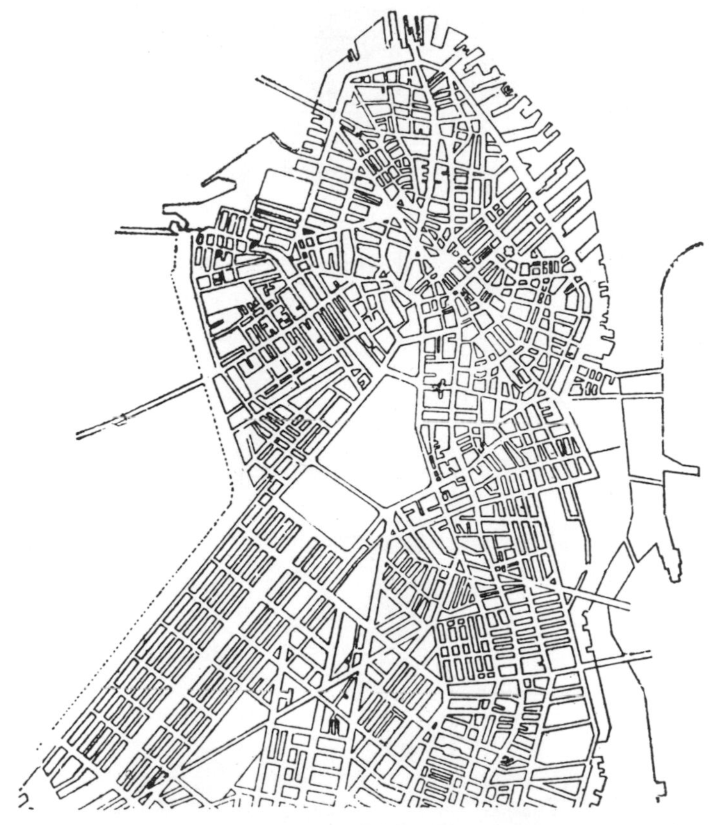

Irregular platting in old sections. Rectangular platting in new sections, especially in Back Bay District, Boston.

by irregular streets or lanes laid out for the convenience of the owner of the tract, and without consideration for the general interests of the city.

Where a plat has been laid out in advance, long, straight streets of even width, at right angles to each other, are found, leaving rectangular blocks for building sites. The older cities with marked modern growth, such as Rome and Athens, New York, Boston and

Baltimore, exhibit almost uniformly an old centre of crooked streets, surrounded by modern rectangular plats, this change proving the general appreciation of the advantages of the rectangular method.

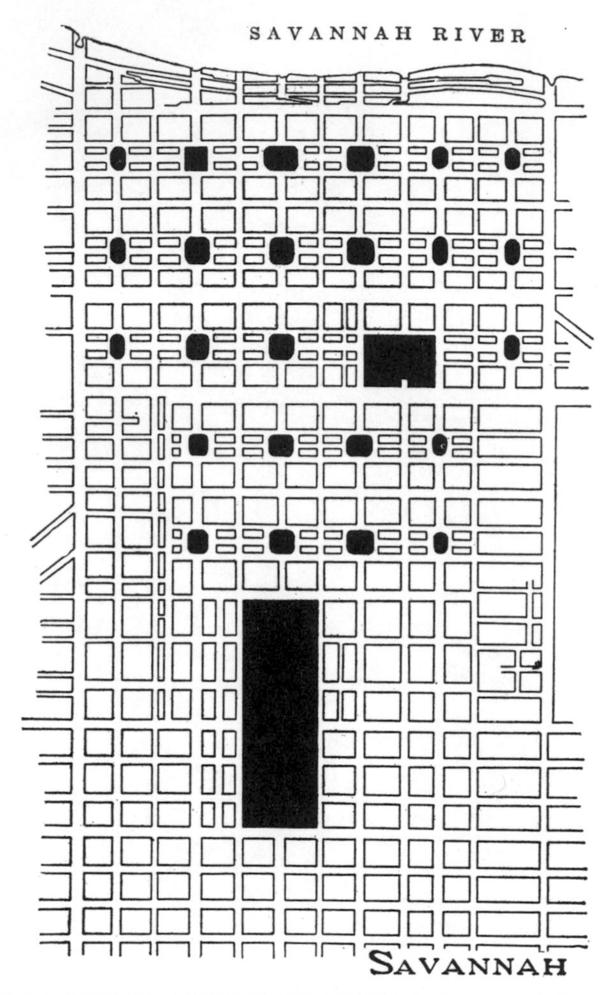

Plat of Savannah showing unusual percentage of park and street area. Plan said to have been derived from Bunyan's description of the Heavenly City.

Some cities, however, have never changed to rectangular platting, among them being Atlanta, Los Angeles, Salem and Lynn.

A number of the older cities originated with a small rectangular plat, surrounded later by rectangular additions, as Philadelphia,

New Orleans, Cleveland and Cincinnati, while the newest cities have generally started with widespread rectangular platting, as Birmingham, Sioux City, Tacoma and Topeka. An exceptional instance would be Memphis, starting with a small rectangular plat, extended

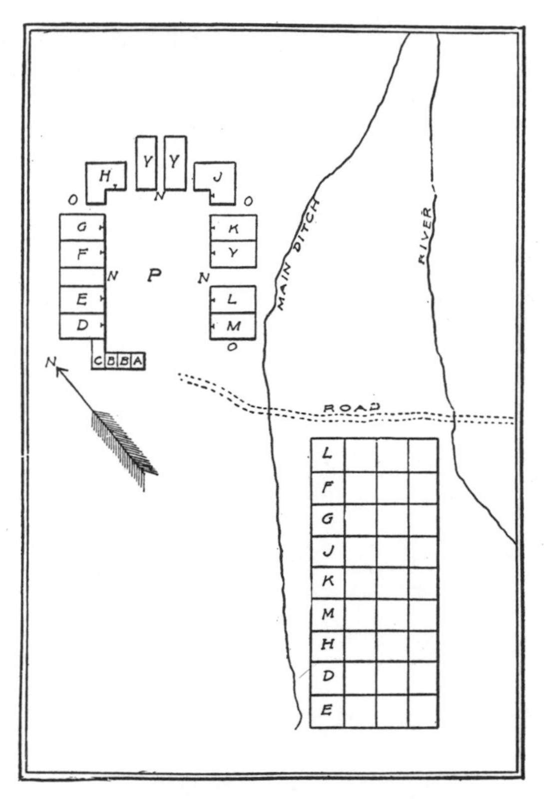

First plat of Los Angeles. Lots around Plaza (marked P) given to settlers; also tracts between irrigating ditch and river, for farming.

later by irregular streets, a reversion recalling the contrast between ancient Alexandria in Egypt with its rectangular plat and modern Alexandria with irregular laying out.

In waterfront cities with rectangular plats the waterfront is normally used as a base, whether straight, curving or broken and irregular, and in inland cities the turnpikes are used as a base. These plats extend to a greater or less distance according to the expectations of the early inhabitants, but finally reach land held according to the section lines of the U. S. Government survey. This change in the direction of holdings commonly changes the direction of the new additions and streets platted, as in Denver, Seattle and Montgomery.

Another variation in rectangular plats is due to the survival of old turnpikes in parts of the city subsequently platted. Many of these old roads are obliterated by platting, but others remain, on account of their convenience for traffic, the important buildings upon them and the fact that land titles are often measured from them, as from Broadway in New York. Of surviving turnpikes, the most

Salt Lake City, about 1860. Large blocks designed for a farming community

common are those which exist in the suburbs, but have been merged into the rectangular streets before reaching the heart of the city, as in Chicago, Philadelphia and Milwaukee. Diagonal turnpikes reaching to the heart of the city still remain in Cleveland and Detroit, and one main turnpike remains in San Francisco, Macon and St. Joseph.

Historically distinct but practically similar to turnpikes are the diagonal streets laid out on the original plat of some cites, such as Washington, Buffalo and Indianapolis. Variations in plats occur where a city is the result of two or more settlements which have grown together and merged, as in Toledo, Montgomery, etc.

The general effect of irregular laying out is to strengthen central growth as opposed to axial growth, quick access to or from the business centre being afforded only by turnpikes. A disadvantage felt later is that as a city expands and quick communication over great distances becomes imperative, vast expense is incurred in widening and straightening streets, this expense being sheer waste due to lack of foresight. Paris under Baron Haussmann spent $250,000,000 on a system of boulevards; London's new Strand im-

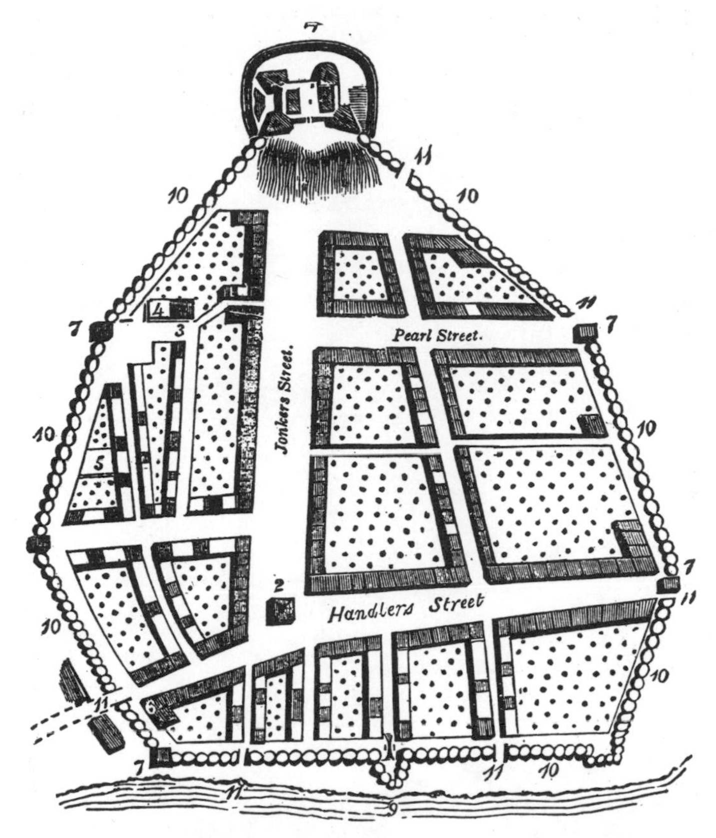

Albany, 1695. Intersection of Handlers and Jonkers Streets, now Broadway and State Street, still the business center of the city.

provements are to cost $33,500,000 (of which $30,000,000 will be refunded from the sale of frontage) and some older American cities, notably Boston, have spent large sums on such work.

The effect of rectangular platting is to permit free movement throughout the city, this being further promoted by the addition of long diagonal streets. The need for diagonal streets depends largely on the shape of the city's site, there being but little use for them in such narrow cities as New York and Boston, while they are of great utility in any city which spreads in all directions over a level area, such as Chicago, Detroit and Buffalo. Washington furnishes an extreme example of diagonal streets, the large proportion of

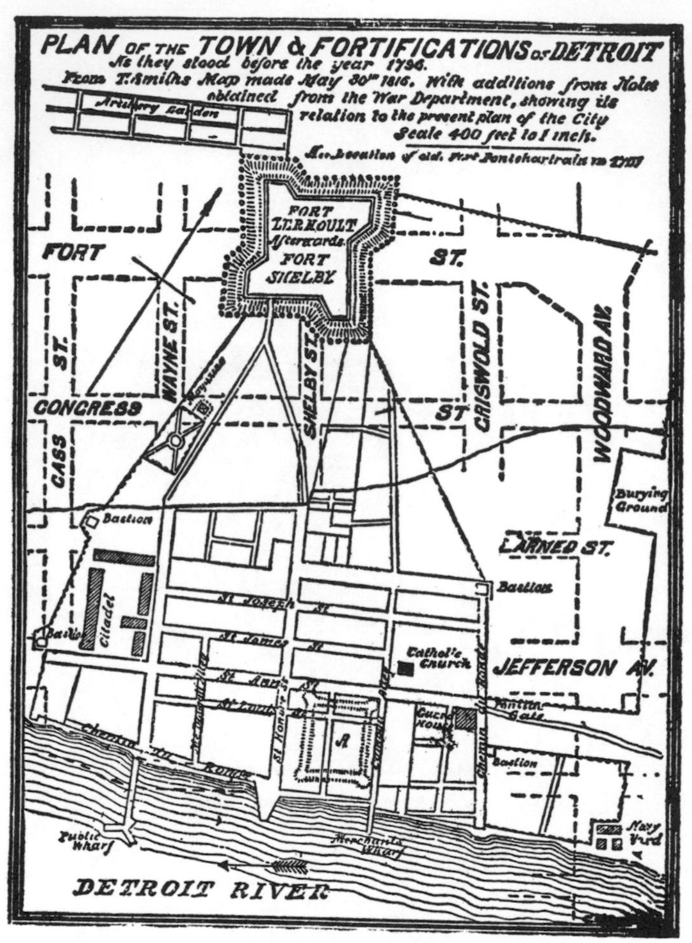

Detroit, 1796. The small first plat near the river and parallel to it has been wiped out by the larger modern platting.

land taken up by streets and squares being suitable to a political city where it would not be economical for a business city.

While early platting is generally made to conform to the needs of the period, in some cases attempts were made to foresee later needs, as in the plat of New York laid out in 1807 from Houston, Eighth and Thirteenth Streets to the Harlem River. Since at that time all commerce was by water, it was reckoned that the chief traffic in New York would necessarily be between the Hudson and the East Rivers, for which reason east and west streets were placed 200 feet apart, while north and south avenues were placed from 600 to 900 feet apart, there being thus fourteen avenues instead of

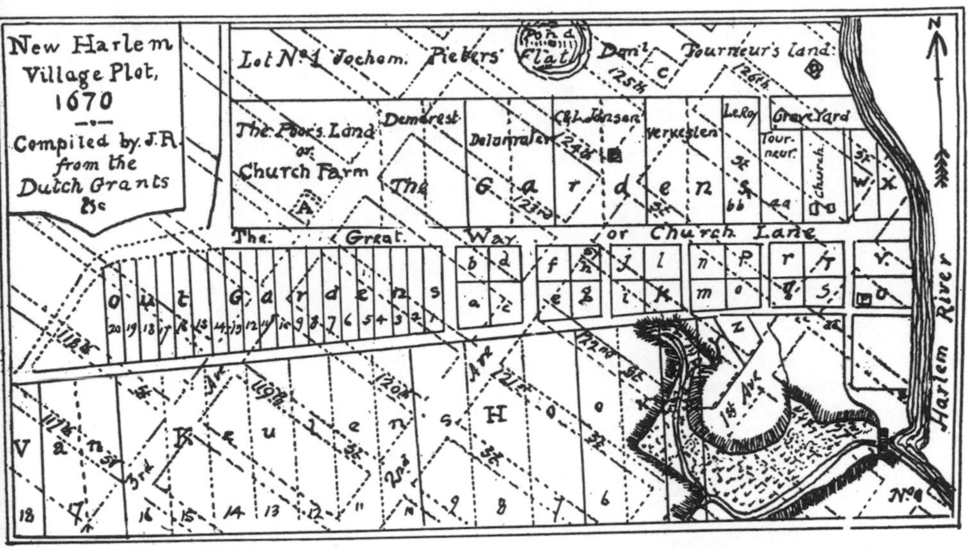

Harlem, 1670. An unusual plat in that the principal street ran at right angles to the river. Old plat wiped out by the New York plat of 1807.

fifty. As a result New York presents in the main the unusual condition of having its business streets running in one direction and its residence streets at right angles. If the Commission had had greater knowledge of cities and could have foreseen the vast growth of New York, they would have realized that the chief internal movement would necessarily be on the line of the longest axis, and the check put upon north and south travel, with the resulting economic loss, would have been avoided. The plats of some cities indicate an attempt on the part of the early platters to locate in advance the centre of the city. In New England and frequently in the South a public square was commonly laid out on which, or facing which, the State and County buildings were erected, also the principal churches and business buildings. Such a square by serving as a barrier to business growth, tended to confine the business part of the

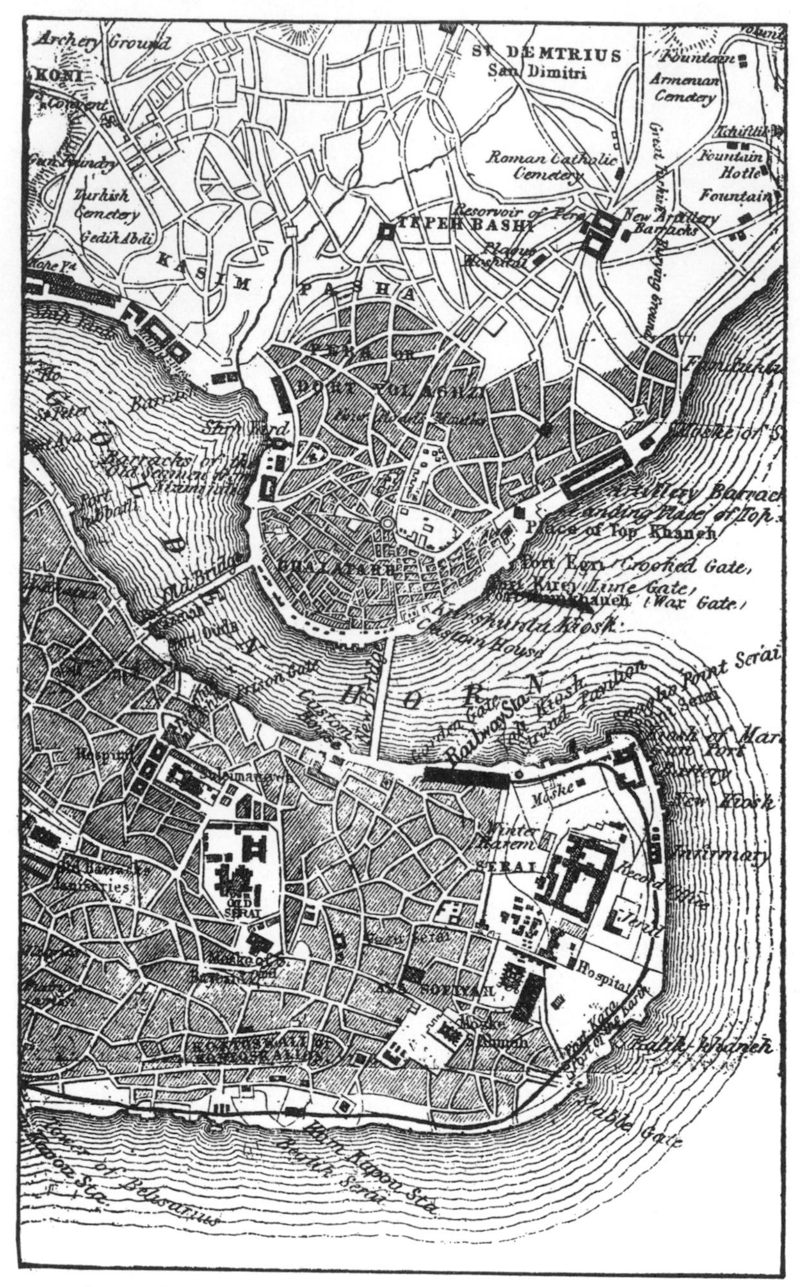

Constantinople. Irregular roads both in city and in outlying district illustrate process by which city is laid out. Buildings are crowded into the large irregular blocks, and small alleys (not shown on map) furnish access.

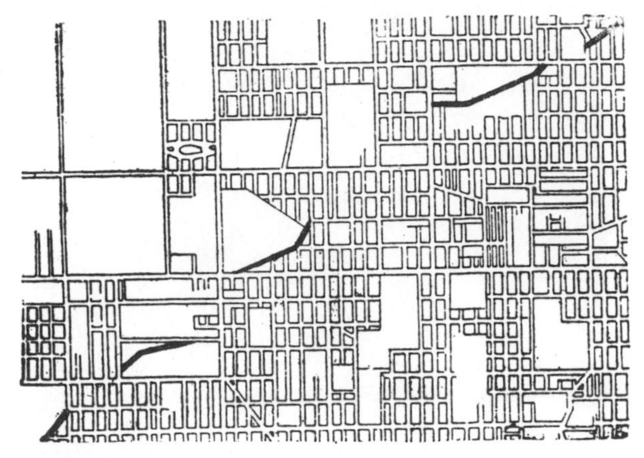

A lost pike. Old Westport-Independence road recently platted out, with growth of residence section. Kansas City.

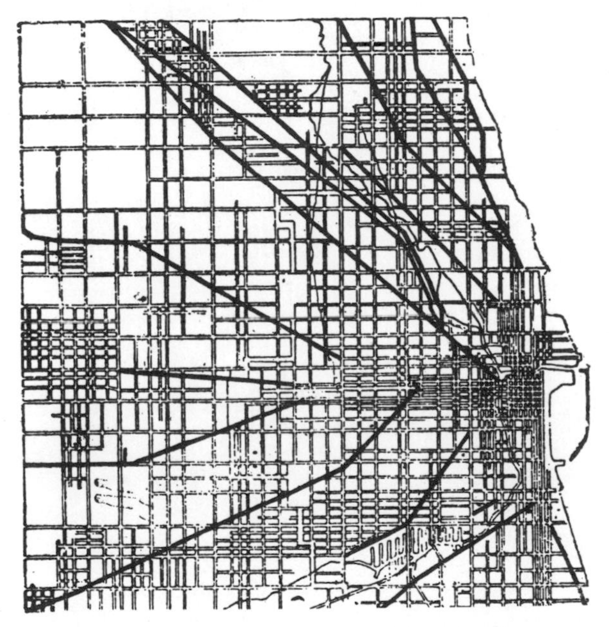

Map of Chicago, showing the surviving turnpikes.

city to that side of the square on which it started, with the exception of such business as spread along the turnpikes, which usually bounded two sides of the square. Another method was to lay out two wide streets at right angles to each other, and strengthen this by locating the County Court House at their intersection, as

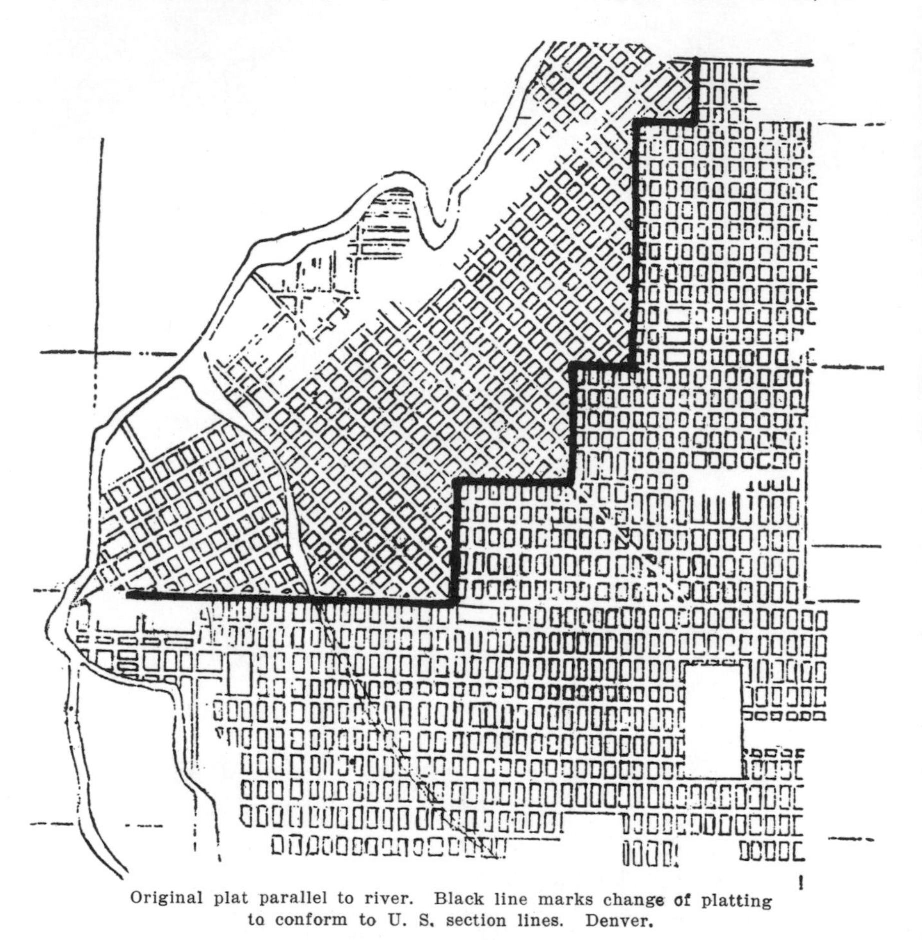

Original plat parallel to river. Black line marks change of platting to conform to U. S. section lines. Denver.

in Philadelphia, with the Court House at the intersection of Broad and Market Streets; in Reading at Penn and Fifth Streets; in Knoxville at Gay and Main Streets; in Terre Haute at Third and Main Streets; in Bay City at Center and Madison Streets, and in Canton at Tuscarora and Market Streets. It is needless to say that such attempts were futile, the business centres of cities depending on more powerful factors than platting and Court Houses. In general, in proportion as a plat is laid out to further the natural lines of a city's growth, it defines and establishes values, and in proportion to its variance with the city's needs it tends to disperse land values and render them unstable.

Turning to a more detailed consideration of plats, variations in

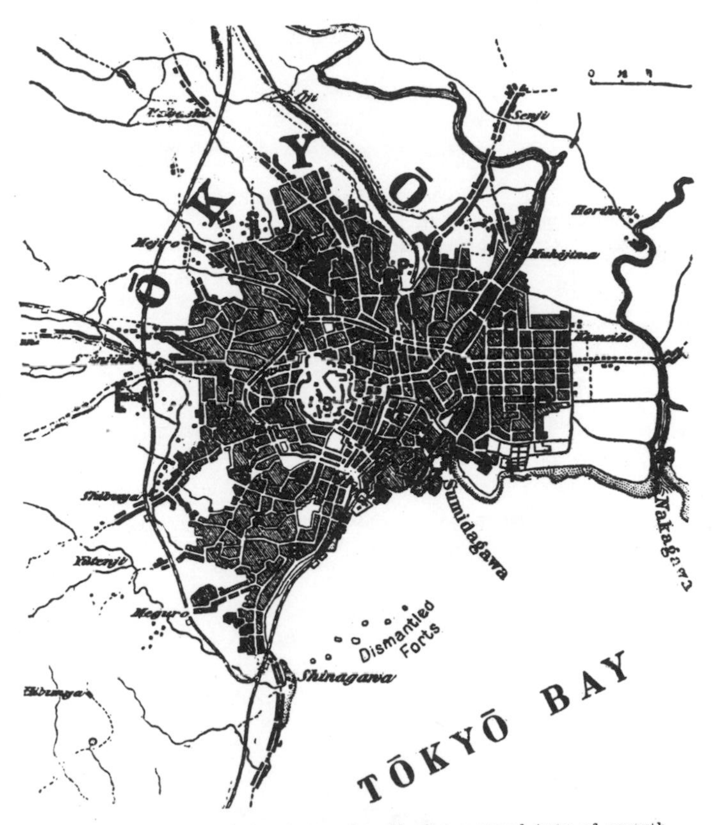

Tokyo, Japan. Example of star-shaped city, normal type of growth.

the width of streets and sizes of blocks involves the proportion of public land used for communication, and of private land used for buildings. In rectangular plats streets usually range in width from forty to eighty feet, sixty feet being a fair average in the newer cities, though every city shows wide variations. There is a common impression that additional width in the street always adds to its value since the wider the street the greater the volume of traffic which ca be accommodated. In a business street width is practically disregarded, but few streets in the world have more traffic than they can carry, additional transportation facilities below ground and above relieving the pressure. In a residence section, however, a wide street is always desirable. A somewhat narrow business street has a slight advantage in facilitating intercourse between the sides of the street, especially as lack of width does not operate to limit the height of buildings, although prominent locations on open squares are sought for some forms of business.

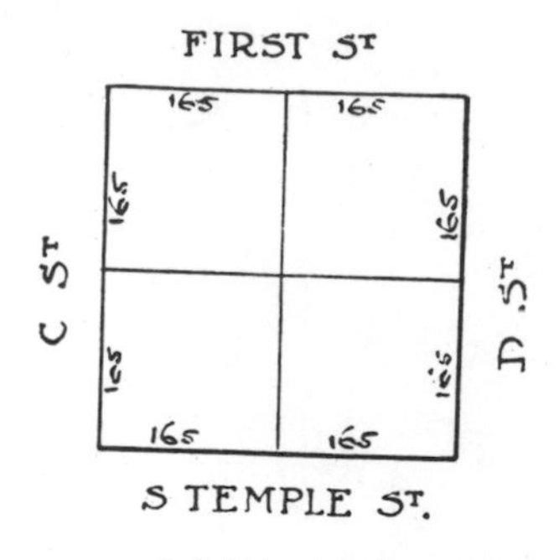

Fig. 1. Simplest form—block divided into quarters.

Alleys are modern developments not found in older cities and usually run parallel to the principal business streets, or the streets which were expected to be the principal business streets when the city was laid out. While in cities of moderate size alleys are useful in furnishing access to the rear of buildings, in the larger cities, where land is closely utilized by means of interior courts and light wells, they are a detriment in interfering with such economic arrangements.

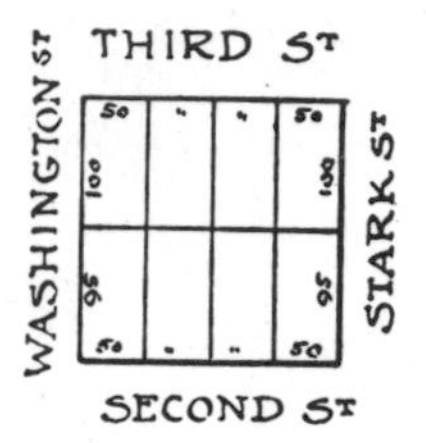

Fig 2. Quarters of block divided in half.

Blocks range in size from 200 feet square to 660 feet square, any depth over 200 to 250 feet involving a waste of land at the interior of the blocks owing to non-accessibility. Salt Lake City with blocks 660 feet square furnishes an aggravated case of loss of value in land by bad platting. The attempts which have

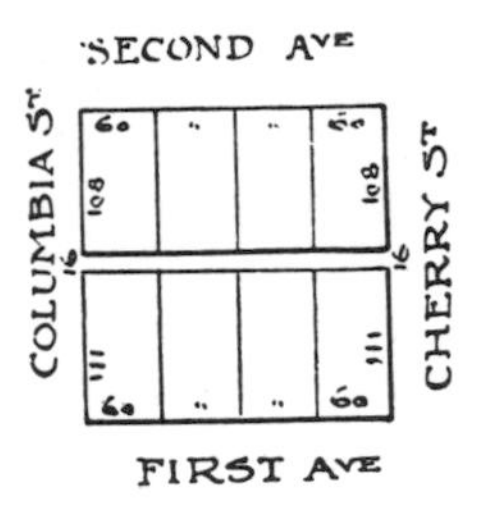

Fig. 3. Same as No. 2, except for alley.

been made to utilize the interior waste land by cutting streets through the large blocks, exhibit a reversion to the primitive methods of individual rather than municipal laying out of streets, these being narrow, irregularly laid out and lacking the vital feature of continuity through the various blocks, thus defeating their avowed object of attracting traffic into the interior of the blocks. The shortsightedness of these owners is due to a supposition that the value of retail business land is based on area instead of on frontage on traffic streets.

The proportion of city area used for streets and alleys ranges from about 35 per cent. in Vienna and New York to 55 per cent. in Washington. The first theoretical aspect of the division of a city's area into public and private land is that the more land given up to streets the greater the dispersion of business and area covered by the city. Limiting this tendency would be a natural increase in the height of buildings, on account of wide streets and greater light and air obtained on the smaller building plots remaining. Practically the proportion between public and private land has but little influence on the density of city population, although there is an economic mean in the proportion between land for communication and land for buildings, which varies according to the utilization of land and which makes itself felt when

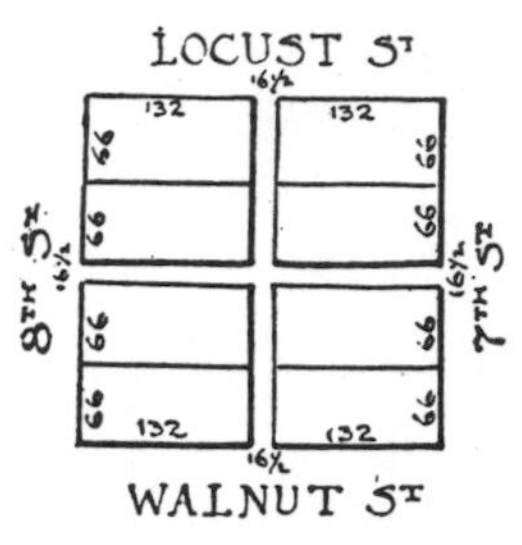

Fig. 4. Same as No. 3, except for double alley.

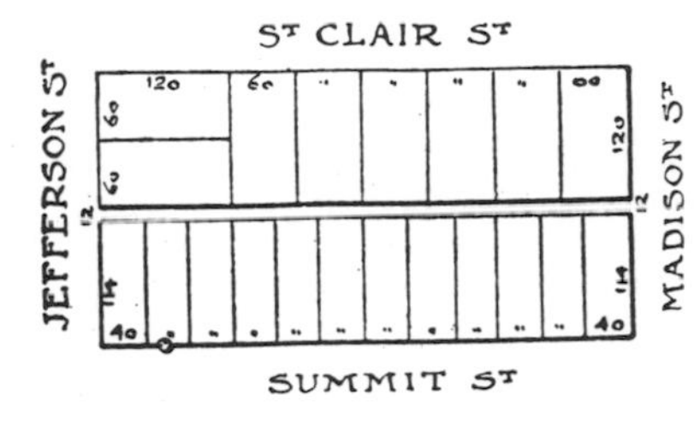

Fig. 5. Variation on No. 3. The more valuable frontage cut into smaller lots. Corner lots face on Jefferson St. because more valuable than St. Clair St.

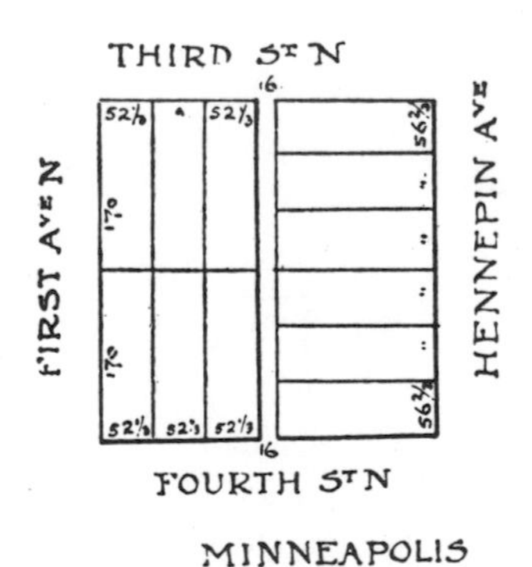

Fig. 6. Variation on No. 3. Lots face the most valuable frontage.

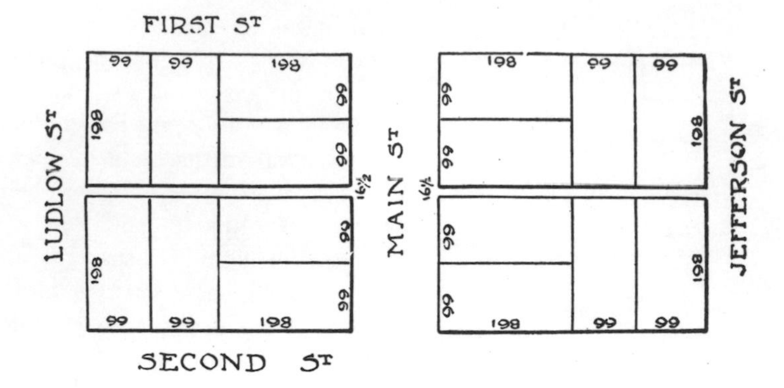

DAYTON. O.

Fig. 7. Lots face Main St., the most valuable frontage, an exception to the general plat.

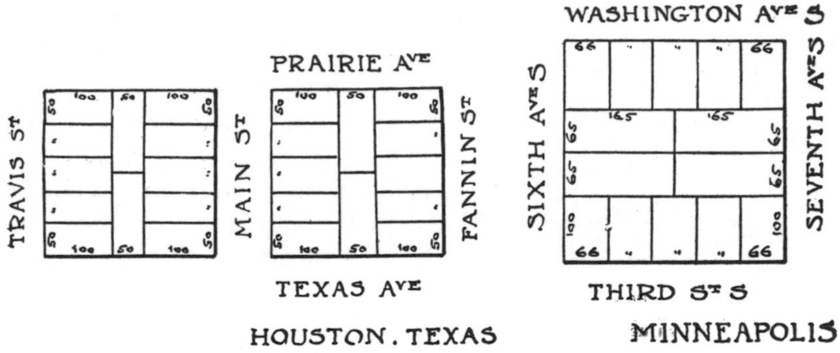

HOUSTON. TEXAS

Fig. 8. Lots face all four streets in proportion to value. Land closely platted.

MINNEAPOLIS

Fig. 9. Similar to No. 8, but a larger block.

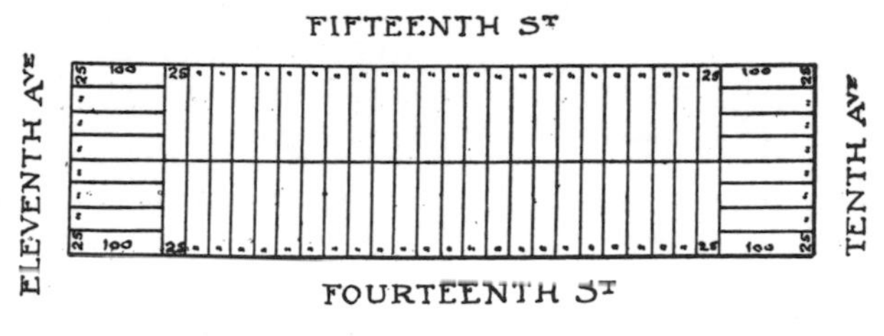

NEW YORK

Fig. 10. Typical long New York block; end lots facing on avenues.

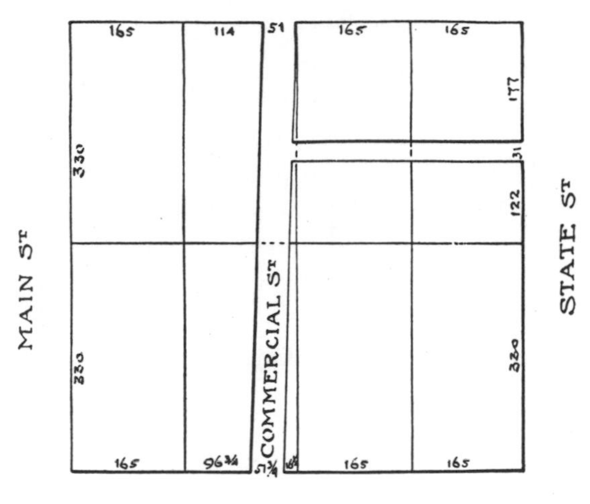

Fig. 11. Irregular cutting through very large block.

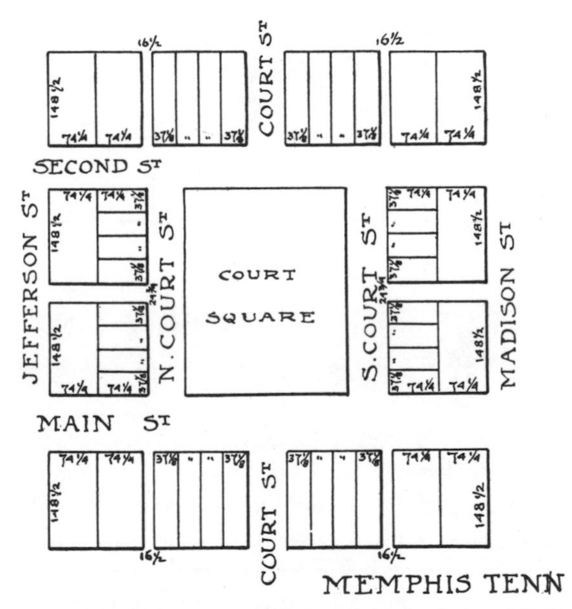

Fig 12. Lots platted to face square, originally designed to be city center.

disregarded in either direction by loss of income.

The unit, both as to the depth and width of lots, from which a plat should be built up, consists of the average shop in the business district and the average dwelling in the residence district. Since the

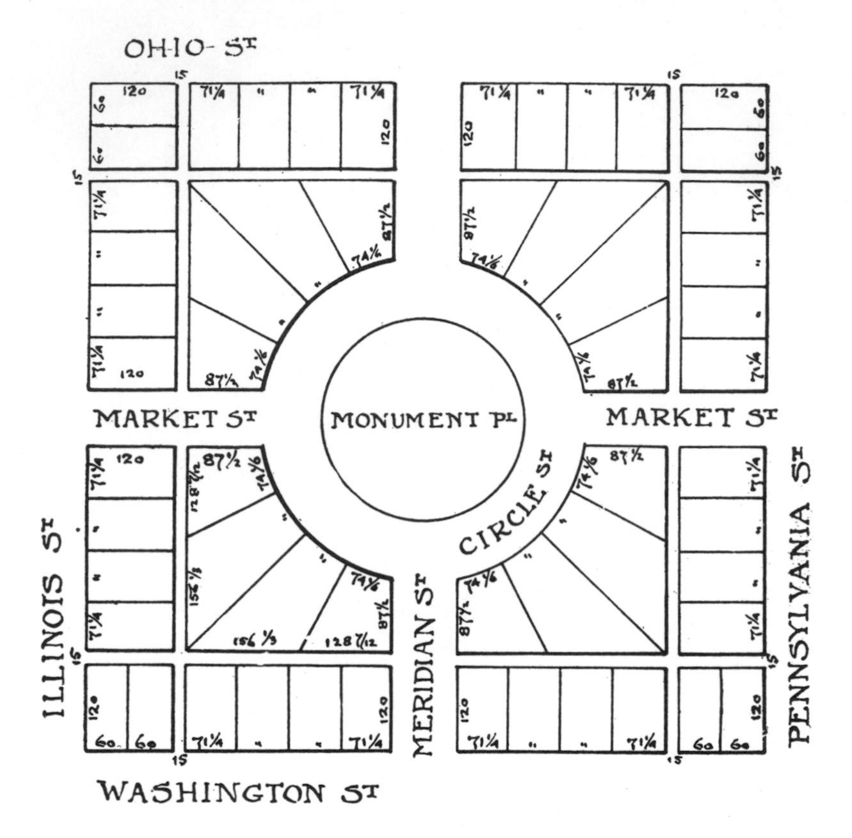

Fig. 13. Waste of land where circle lots deepest. Also monument interferes with traffic in both directions and injures both streets.

growth of cities leads normally to the ultimate conversion of residence land into business land, a uniform system of platting suitable for business purposes throughout the entire city is generally preferable. Such a system need not necessarily lead to small holdings in the residence sections, although it has a tendency in that direction.

The average depth utilized by shops varies from 30 or 40 feet for cheap shops up to 70 or 80 feet for high-class shops, with some department stores 200 to 400 feet deep. The average shop was formerly limited in depth by the necessity of obtaining light from each end, but this limitation has been removed by the use of artificial light in the day time. Allowing 30 or 40 feet in the rear for light and air, we have a normal depth of 100 to 120 feet for a lot, or a total depth, including an alley, of 200 to 250 feet to the block. Very long blocks are much less disadvantageous than very deep ones, the unfavorable feature here being that shops in the middle

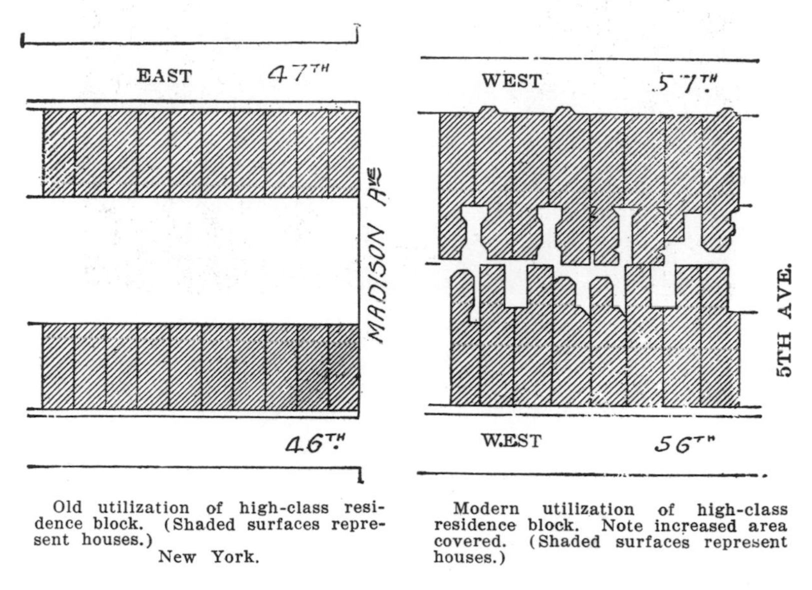

Old utilization of high-class residence block. (Shaded surfaces represent houses.)
New York.

Modern utilization of high-class residence block. Note increased area covered. (Shaded surfaces represent houses.)

of the long fronts are difficult of access, as with the side streets in New York from Fourteenth Street up.

Office buildings can utilize a greater depth than shops, extending from 100 to 150 feet, and as to wholesale and warehouse buildings, light and air being almost unnecessary, the only limitation of depth is that of convenience in handling goods.

Residences erected in blocks are usually two or three rooms deep, covering 50 to 70 feet, so that, with an allowance for light and air, 100 to 120 feet is a desirable depth for residence lots. Where residence land is most valuable it is economized in the same way as with office buildings, the entire area being built on except for such light wells as are necessary or required by the building laws. In some of the best residence sections of smaller cities, lots of extra depth are found, permitting the dwellings to be set far back from the

Planned as interior street, in effect an alley through the most valuable block in Salt Lake City. Frontage practically worthless.

Examples of too wide street. Street narrowed from 100 feet to 56 feet. Sidewalks moved to edges of driveway. Expense of maintaining driveway reduced one-half and desirable parking effects obtained. Macon, Ga.

street, as with Euclid Avenue, Cleveland, where the lots on one side of the street are 900 feet deep, and Meridian Avenue in Indianapolis, where the lots on one side of the street are 400 feet deep. In the outskirts of small cities where land is cheap and but a small proportion of the land is built upon, great depth is customarily made use of for gardens, the deep lots being cut by additional streets as further demand for building land arises.

As to width of lots, these vary in the smaller cities from 20 to 25 feet for mechanics' homes, 40 to 60 feet for medium class residences or small shops, and 100 to 150 feet for high-class residences or the largest business buildings. In the largest cities residence lots run from 12 to 25 feet and business lots from 25 to 50 feet, with larger plots of 100 feet frontage or more used for large office buildings, shops, hotels, theatres or costly residences, the general rule being the larger the city the smaller the average holding of land.

A marked effect of the subdivision of land into small lots occurs in the largest cities when large plots are needed, such plots having greatly increased value, technically known as "plottage" value. From one standpoint this represents the "hold-up" cost of securing the last few lots of a plot, the plans concerning which almost invariably leaking out and advantage being taken of purchasers' necessities.

CHAPTER V.

Directions of Growth

THE FIRST feature of any settlement to be noted is its correspondence with external influences, the first buildings of a commercial city clustering around the point of origin, whether a wharf, railroad station or turnpike intersection, in order to handle the traffic from the outside world.

In a waterfront city the first line of growth is normally along the

Geneva in 1687. First streets parallel to the water front.

shore, both because additional docks and buildings opposite them start an axis of travel parallel to the waterfront, and also because the bank of a river or harbor furnishes a natural highway for the first settlers, the Strand in London being the typical first street of a waterfront city. Thus the first business street of New York was Pearl Street, originally on the shore line of the East River; of Chicago, Water Street, on the edge of the Chicago River; of Boston, Washington Street, then in part on the shore line; of

Savannah, Bay Street; of Bridgeport, Water Street, etc., these streets being now in most cases a number of blocks from the water, owing to the extension of land by filling.

A not uncommon variation in this normal development has

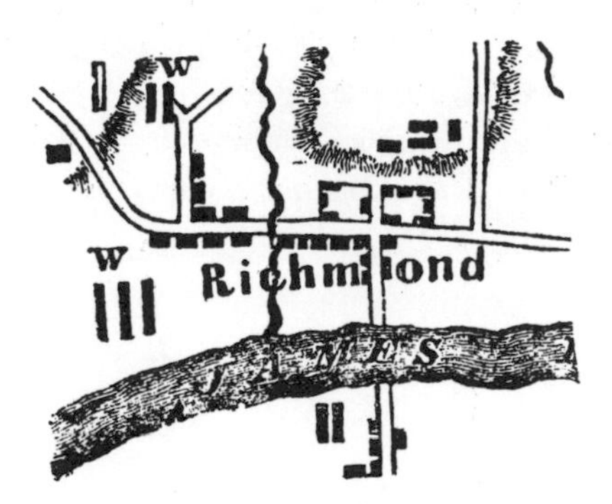

Richmond in 1781. Showing the first buildings on Main Street.

occurred where a creek emptying into the river or harbor made a sheltered landing-place, whose traffic brought business buildings on either side. When the size of ships was so increased that the creek became useless it was filled up, the business street, however, remain-

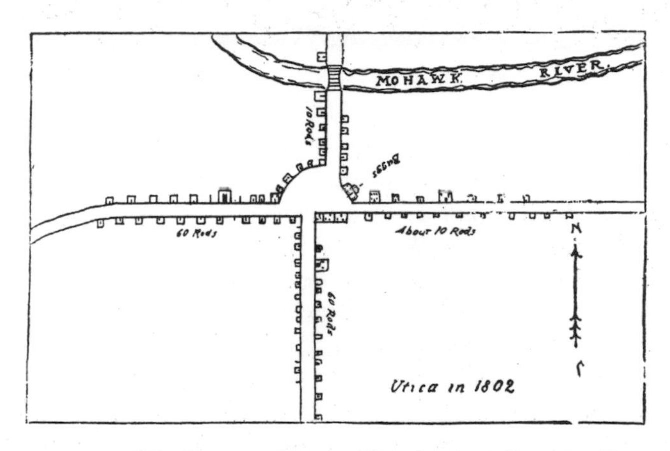

Utica in 1802. Typical start of a city at intersecting turnpikes.

ing, as with Broad Street in New York; Dock Street in Philadelphia, and Canal Street in New Orleans. Where the topography of the waterfront, either because of shallow water at each end or of cliffs along the banks, is such that only one good approach to the water exists, the first business street will normally extend back from the waterfront up the hollow between the hills, as at Evansville, Montgomery and Kansas City.

In the case of an inland town there may be four or more directions of growth along the lines of the intersecting turnpikes. Where an inland city originates from a railroad, the railroad station takes the place of the wharves of a waterfront city, and the first direction of growth is along the turnpike leading to the largest body of productive farming land. Since this usually lies along the valley through

Cleveland, 1796. The first streets run up the hill from the river docks.

which the railroad runs, the first axis of growth is commonly parallel to the railroad. Wherever a town is found in which the railroad station is evidently apart from the organic structure of the town, it is clear that the town existed before the railroad reached it.

The chief exceptions to these general principles would be where inland villages arose before their turnpikes were of importance, as with Lancaster growing up about a spring; Syracuse near the salt wells; Indianapolis artificially laid out, but with the settlers shifted over the city's site, first, by absence of timber on part of the city plat, next by the terminus of the canal, and next by the location of the National Pike.

In their methods of growth cities conform always to biological laws, all growth being either central or axial. In some cities central growth occurs first and in others axial growth, but all cities illustrate both forms of growth and in all cases central growth includes some axial growth, and axial growth some central growth. Central growth consists of the clustering of utilities around any point of attraction and is based on proximity, while axial growth is the result of transportation facilities and is based on accessibility. A continual contest exists between axial growth, pushing out from the centre along transportation lines, and central growth, constantly following and obliterating it, while new projections are being made further out the various axes. The normal result of axial and central growth is a star-shaped city, growth extending first along the main thoroughfares radiating from the centre, and later filling in the parts lying

Portland, Ore. Showing first growth along river bank.

between. The modifications of the shape of cities come chiefly from topography, the lesser influences being an uneven development of some one factor of growth or individual ownership of land.

Turning first to axial growth, the frame-work of a city is laid down by its water courses, turnpikes and railroads. Of these, the turnpikes in the older cities are of chief importance. Before the days of railroads these controlled so much outside traffic that their city ends became the principal business streets, and many still maintain their supremacy. For example, Broadway in New York was part of the old Albany turnpike which runs on to Montreal; Washington Street in Boston was the turnpike to New York, which in passing through Providence was known as Westminster Street; Main Street in Hartford was the New Haven turnpike, which continued north of Hartford as the Albany and Windsor turnpikes; Montgomery

Street in Jersey City was the through road from New York to the south, which, continuing out Newark Avenue, runs through Newark as Broad Street, and so on to Philadelphia; the National Pike, built from Washington to the west one hundred years ago, runs through Wheeling as Market Street, Columbus as Broad Street, Indianapolis as Washington Street, Terre Haute as Main Street, and so on; and in Kansas City Main Street was the old Sante Fe trail, running a thousand miles from the Missouri River to Sante Fe.

Turnpikes are the natural outlets for residences forced away

Wheeling, W. Va., in 1845. Showing first growth parallel to river. The road over the hill is the National Pike.

from the business centre and in small towns attract the inhabitants by the human interest and protection of the passing travel. Growth along turnpikes continues to a point where the inconvenience of living so far out of town more than offsets the attractions of the turnpike when back streets are laid out.

Steam railroads affect city land in three ways: First, by their terminals; second, by their lines as barriers to growth or communication; and, third, by their lines as influencing land immediately adjacent. The central effect of a passenger depot in a small city is to attract cheap hotels and shops, such abnormal cases as the vacant lots opposite the Union depots in Toledo and New Haven being due to railroad ownership of the land. In the larger cities high-class hotels gather near the principal depots, as in New York and

Boston, and in England, where they are frequently built as a part of the railroad station itself.

The axial effect of railroad depots is of great importance in the

Cincinnati in 1810. First houses along the river bank.

smaller towns, where the depot constitutes one of the strongest single forces attracting traffic within the city. The distribution of this axial effect depends upon whether the travel to and from the

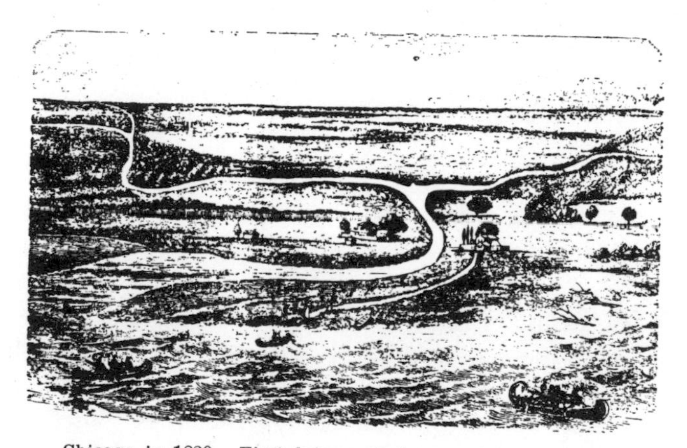

Chicago in 1820. First houses at the mouth of the river.

depot is concentrated on one principal street, or whether the streams of travel pass through a large number of streets. Ordinarily the railroad terminal occupies so much area and blocks so many streets that it is most conveniently approached by one street. The axial effect of a depot is more easily noted when it is located a few blocks from a through traffic street than if located on such a street, the travel off the through street being then directly due to the depot and not being mingled with the general travel. In some cases a depot blocks the end or furnishes the beginning of a street which would for other reasons have been a good street but which is greatly strengthened by the depot, as with 17th Street in Denver. Freight depots are commonly a part of passenger terminals and attract warehouses, heavy wholesalers and tenements.

The restraining effect of railroads, whether main or belt lines, varies according to the territory traversed. Where a railroad runs through a business section at grade, it limits communication between the divided sections and tends to concentrate business on one side of the line. Where a railroad in a business section is carried below or above grade, its effect is minimized. In a poor residence section a

Dawson City, Alaska, 1899. Showing

railroad has but little effect, but in a high-class residence section it forms a nuisance which good residences shun. Added to the noise and cinders of passing trains is the fact that the railroad attracts factories and warehouses, which are also nuisances in a residence district. In some instances the railroad travels along the line of a small creek or gully within the city, which has already kept land values down, so that the railroad has but little added effect, as with the greater part of the Belt Line in Kansas City. If the railroad is in a deep cut, its limiting effect on good residences is diminished, as in Chattanooga and St. Paul. In some cities demand for land in the good residence district is so great that the residence district is projected beyond the encircling railroad with little fall in values, as in Louisville and Richmond, where handsome residences are built adjacent to the railroad. In New York, the N. Y. Central R. R. on Park Avenue between 42d and 56th Street holds the high-class residences on the west side of the track, the east side of the track being ruined by absence of approach, the only communication being by the elevated foot bridges. From 56th Street north the tracks enter the tunnel and their effect is lessened, the only objection being the vent holes in Park Avenue. In all cities railroads detach great slices of city area, in which they alter utilizations and values much as important water courses do.

The effect of railroads on adjacent frontage is to prevent its use for either shops or residences, the chief exception to this being in small towns where the street facing the railroad often starts as the principal business street, this condition still surviving in Syracuse.

Water fronts, if navigable, invite commerce, resulting in docks

axial growth along river bank.

and warehouses, and away from the city centre attract factories. If not navigable and not bordered by railroads, and if the land is not low, they attract residences, as in Chicago, north of the Chicago River; in Charleston, and formerly in New York, when the best residences faced the Battery Park. Where the land rises sharply fifty or more feet above the river level, so that the railroads and traffic along the water are not seen or heard on the hill above, residences are attracted, as in the Riverside Drive district in New York; the Summit Avenue district in St. Paul; the Independence Avenue district in Kansas City, and the Walnut Hill district in Cincinnati.

Turning to central growth, this has two aspects, first the main general growth in all directions from the point of origin, second the growth from various sub-centres within the city, such as trans-

Washington about 1840, looking up Pennsylvania Avenue from the White House to the Capitol.

portation termini, public buildings, exchanges, factories, hotels, etc.

The first and simplest form of central growth is that of aggregation or adding of buildings one after another along the streets leading from the centre of the city. The first dwellings in a village are located near the business buildings, so that the merchants can walk to and from their business, and so great is the power of

Broad street canal of New York in 1650. Location of early mercantile houses and the first exchange.

inertia that even in the smallest villages the few stores find it advantageous to be close together.

The influence of public buildings on the structure of a commercial city is small, unless such a commercial city is also a national capital, as with London and Paris. Where a city is wholly a political city, as is Washington, the public buildings largely determine the structure of the city. The smaller public buildings found in all cities, such as the Post Office and City Hall, have considerable influence in determining the line of early growth, but are of constantly diminishing importance as the other factors of a city's life

Richmond, Va., about 1840. Showing growth along river and up gradual slope to the south.

become stronger, so that not infrequently the public building which created a street in time becomes a detriment to it. It is easy to find public buildings badly located which have no effect on the city's structure, as the Post Office in Chattanooga, the County Court Houses in Salt Lake City, Kansas City, Seattle and Tacoma, and the State Capital in Salt Lake City. If the City Hall includes a public market for the sale of vegetables, fruit, meat, etc., this being similar to a large shop attracts much daily travel, a good example being in Knoxville. In some cities, as in Columbus and Dayton, O., farmers sell their products from wagons on certain streets of the city on market days. When this was first instituted the shop-keepers

Farnam Street, Omaha, 1863. Old buildings replaced by modern ones, leaving but few traces of first growth.

St. Paul in 1868. City started at deep water and high bank, making good steamboat landing. Climbed hill to "Seven Corners," then grew east on lower level towards railroad station.

on these streets feared injury to their trade and secured the passage of a city ordinance prohibiting it. Finding later that they had lost patronage by the removal of the farmers' wagons, they petitioned for their return, this experience showing the value to shop-keepers of massing people in front of their stores, even though the new attracting force consists of competitive sellers. The practice of surrounding public buildings with large grounds is a common one, by which their influence is nullified, the net effect being similar to that of a small park. Such a small park, even though including a public building, makes a bad break on a through business street, injuring especially

Water front of Seattle, 1878. No commerce demanded docks, so water front was bulkheaded. Two new streets have since been laid out over the water, and continuous docks built.

the adjacent property on the same side of the street. It may sometimes slightly enhance the value of the business property facing it by concentrating travel on that side of the street, and in the largest cities furnishes a desirable outlook for high office buildings. The most detrimental effect of such a public building in a small park is felt in the early stages of a city, where the park checks the extension of the business centre. A public building surrounded by a park, if located in a residence section, tends to attract good residences, the outlook for the park more than off-setting what travel comes to the public building.

To summarize the effect of public buildings, if located at or near the old business centre they tend to maintain central strength in their first location, as in Boston, New York, Philadelphia and Chicago. This is the normal case. The first exceptions would be where public buildings are located at a moderate distance from the centre, where the tendency is to draw business in their direction, and the second where they have been so misplaced as to fail to have any influence.

Macon, Ga. The point of origin, where bridge crossed from East Macon, which was first settled. This frontage, formerly the highest priced in the city, now worth about $10 a front foot.

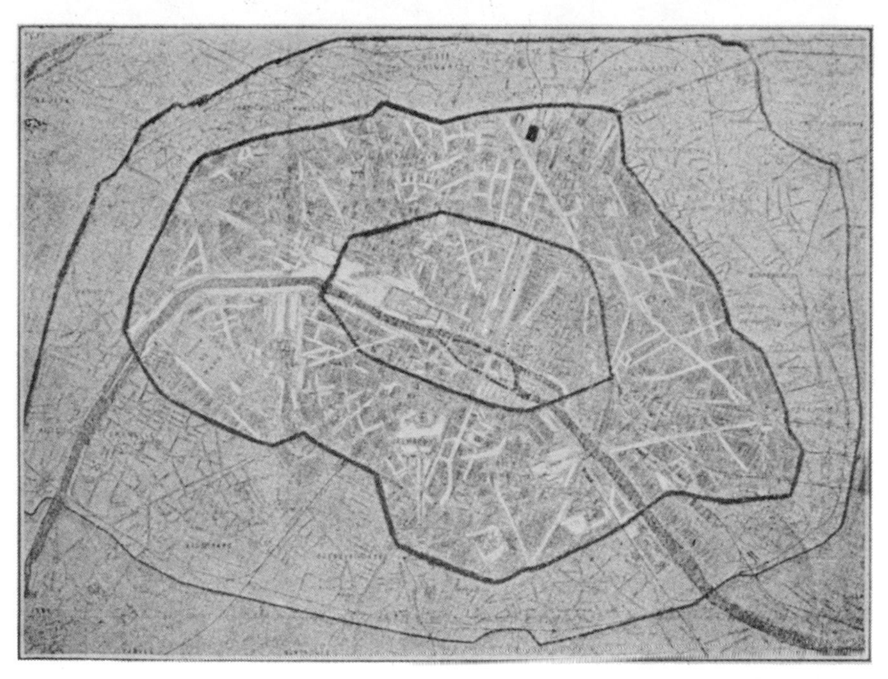

Paris. Central growth exhibited by successive encircling boulevards.

Brooklyn. Illustrates growth along the axis of the Long Island R. R.

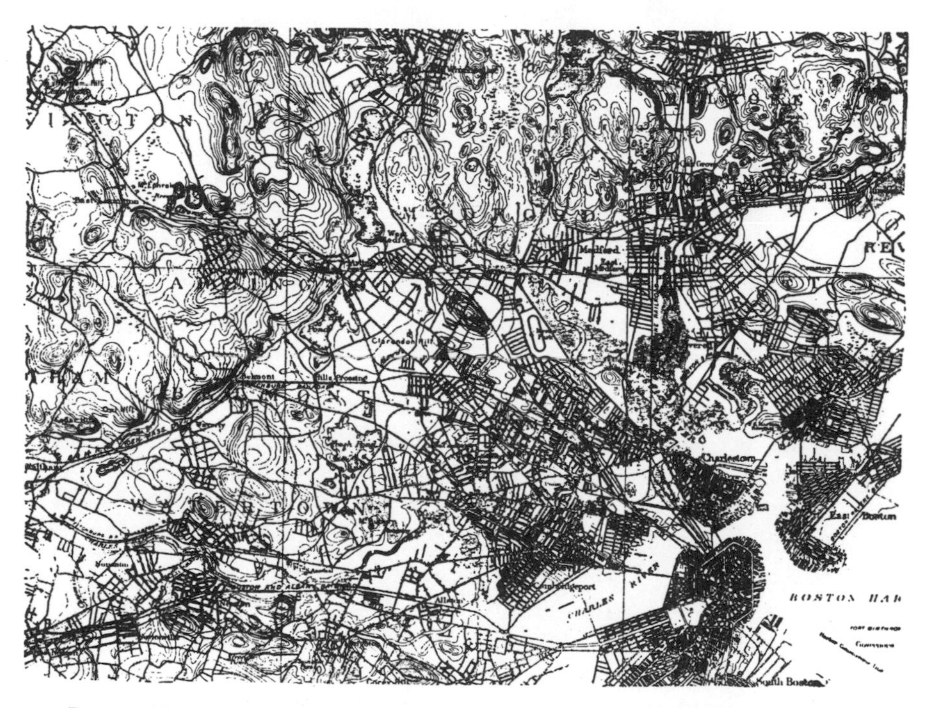

Boston. Illustrates central growth at points on railroad axis, issuing from the city.

Arising later in the life of a city, but in time acquiring more central influence than any other factor, are the Exchanges, such as the Stock Exchange, Produce Exchange, Cotton Exchange, Coffee Exchange, Wool Exchange, etc. The New York Stock Exchange is the strongest single influence maintaining the financial section. The proposition considered some years ago of moving the Stock Exchange above Prince Street, and on another occasion to 14th Street, if accomplished would have removed all the Stock Exchange brokers and the majority of the Banks and Trust Companies, private bankers, Safe Deposit Companies and lawyers, with disastrous results

Fine old Southern residence separated from its neighborhood by railroad cutting. Value of land and building destroyed. Montgomery, Ala

on land values in the financial section. The leading Exchange varies in different cities according to the dominant form of business. The Board of Trade, handling the grain business, is the leading Exchange of Chicago and Minneapolis; the Cotton Exchange of New Orleans, Savannah and Mobile; and the Mining Exchange of Denver and Colorado Springs.

Factories create sub-centres, most distinct when on the outskirts of cities, by causing the erection of laborers' cottages near the factory, which in turn attract small shops and public and semi-public buildings. Where factories are erected within the built-up section of the city, their central effect mingles with that of other factors, but attracts tenements near at hand.

Charleroux, France. Illustrates first lines of buildings along roads, which form large irregular blocks, later subdivided.

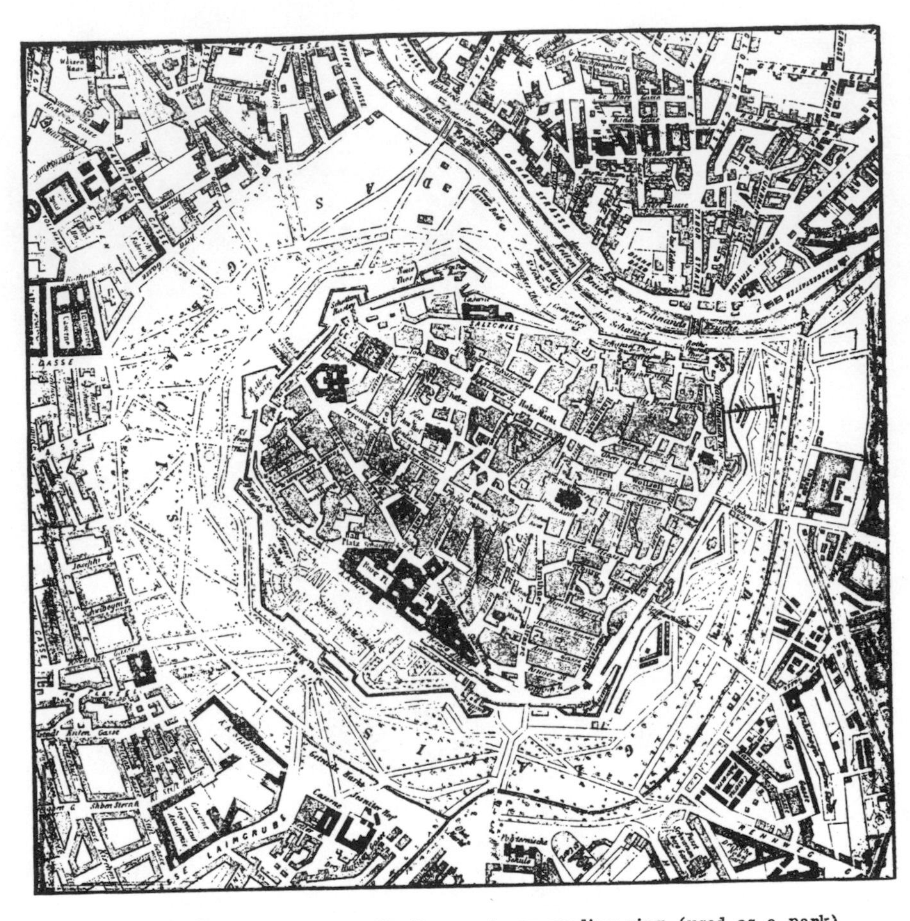

Vienna, 1873. Showing fortifications and surrounding ring (used as a park), which made the old business center, in effect, an island.

Vienna, 1898. Showing ring outside the old fortifications, platted into regular blocks. These now highly improved with municipal and public buildings, apartment houses, &c.

In all growth, central or axial, great or small, the vital feature is continuity, the universal tendency being to add on buildings one by one, of the same general character as those which preceded them. Lack of continuity from whatever cause explains many of the greatest disappointments in anticipated real estate movements, such as for example the failure of the west side in New York, when first developed, to attract fine residences. While growth in general is continuous, in detail it may hasten on, leaving vacant places behind, especially where rapid transit draws it, the stations of the elevated railroad on the west side at 72d, 81st, 93d, 104th and 116th Streets being starting points in new territory from which growth took place in all directions.

Atlanta. Example of star-shaped city.
(See page 47.)

CHAPTER VI.

Distribution of Utilities

THE PHYSICAL evolution of a large city from a small one results not only from increased population and added industries, but also from continual specialization in business and differentiation in social grades. The first step is the separation between business and dwellings, the original buildings used for business below and dwellings above being replaced by separate business and residence buildings. Later the social activities in educational, charitable and recreational lines become organized and evidence themselves in schools, hospitals, theatres and clubs, increasing diversity of function resulting in increased diversity of structure. Analyzing city land according to its utilization, it may be divided into three main classes, that used for business, that for residences and that for public or semi-public buildings.

Business land may be subdivided into that used for distribution—retail or wholesale stores and railroads; that used for administration—banking and office property; and that used for production—manufacturing property.

Residence land may be subdivided into that occupied by a single tenant, ranging from the cottage to the palace, and that occupied by more than one tenant, ranging from tenements to apartments and hotels.

Land used for public or semi-public buildings includes that used by the Post Office, City Hall, County Court House, etc., and by all such institutions as asylums, hospitals, churches, libraries, museums, clubs, etc.

The locations sought by these utilities and the reasons therefor seem to be as follows: Retail stores either cluster at the business center or follow out traffic streets. In retailing the buyer necessarily seeks the seller, but since in all forms of trade it is the seller who is anxious to promote business the retailer facilitates his possible customers by placing his shop where the largest number of them would pass even though his shop were not there. Here he utilizes his shop windows and signs to draw customers into his shop, the two elements of convenience of location and advertising advantage working hand in hand.

Wholesaling may be divided into two main classes: First, wholesaling of objects of great weight or bulk but relatively small value, which seeks locations near transportation lines or termini for economy of handling, the selling being done by travelling salesmen or by selling agencies located in the business centre; and, second, wholesaling of articles of small bulk but high value in the retail-wholesale way, that is, making up an order including a variety of objects for the

Second Street, Seattle, in 1876, looking south. Lots which sold in 1860 for $10 now bring $120,000. None of the original buildings survive.

trade only—which seeks locations near their chief customers, the retail stores. Here the ability to quickly supply a small order of mixed goods is sufficiently important to induce them to pay considerable rents.

Railroads in striving for passenger traffic project their passenger terminals as far as possible towards the business centre of a city. Economy of handling freight locates the freight depots either near the docks for interchange of freight or near the heavy business houses.

In the largest cities a separate section evolves devoted to office buildings, whose ground floors are utilized by banks, trust companies, insurance companies, etc., and whose offices are rented to brokers, lawyers, architects, etc., the location of such an administrative district being usually the result of slow growth around old institutions.

Manufacturing follows similar lines to wholesaling, the production of articles of great weight or bulk and small value seeking the waterfronts or railroads away from the centre of the city, both for economy in handling the product and because, requiring a large area for a low utilization, they must have cheap land. The manufacture of light articles of high value or that which consists of the final combination or finishing of products seeks the wholesale or retail stores which form their customers. In such manufacturing the seller seeks

Memphis levee, showing use of waterfront where marked changes of river levels occur. Absence of docks prevents localizing of river business, and resulting effects on city structure.

the buyer and sells by sample, so that a location with an advertising value is not imperative, but the requirement of constant visits to customers and the ability to supply small articles quickly causes such manufacturers to pay considerable rents.

In general the basis of the distribution of all business utilities is purely economic, land going to the highest bidder and the highest bidder being the one who can make the land earn the largest amount. We may note that the better the location the more uses to which it can be put, hence the more bidders for it.

On the other hand, the basis of residence values is social and not economic—even though the land goes to the highest bidder—the rich selecting the locations which please them, those of moderate means living as near by as possible, and so on down the scale of wealth, the poorest workmen taking the final leavings, either adjacent to such nuisances as factories, railroads, docks, etc., or far out of the city. Certain features appear to attract the wealthy in selecting their residence districts, among these being nearness to parks, a good approach from the business centre, not too near nor yet too far, a moderate elevation if obtainable, favorable transportation facilities, despite the fact that the rich ride in their own carriages and automobiles, and above all absence of nuisances. Having selected a district the wealthy make it their own by erecting handsome residences, making good street improvements, restricting against nuisances, and finally and of chief importance living there themselves, the value of residence land varying directly according to the social standing of its occupants. The main consideration in the individual selection of a residence location is the desire to live among one's friends or among those whom one desires to have for friends; for which reason there will be as many residence neighborhoods in a city as there are social strata. In securing a home in a good residence section a man secures safe, healthy and attractive conditions for his family to live under, and, in the smaller cities, desirable social life, these social considerations explaining the strong pressure in all cities towards the best residence sections. The contrast should be noted that business property is selected by the man from an economic standpoint, and residence property by the woman from a social standpoint. Social growth and pressure is upwards from class to class, all ranks being continually recruited from below—as well as dropping members from time to time—and the ultimate aim in residence location is to be as close as possible to those of the highest social position.

Where residences contain more than one tenant, whether tenements, flats, apartments or hotels, the basis of value is economic and conforms closely to the principles governing business property. The hotels of various classes seek locations similar to the retail stores of the same classes on convenient traffic streets which advertise them. The highest class apartment hotels seek locations on or near such traffic streets as run through or near the fashionable districts, the rents being dependent both upon fashion and on the character and service of the building. Below this grade the various classes of flats seek locations for the convenience of their tenants, tending to draw nearer and nearer to their tenants' places of business, until finally we reach tenements crowded among the factories where their occupants work.

Turning to the main central growth of cities, a successful business at or near the city centre which requires more space can secure it either by acquiring adjoining ground, by building higher in the air, or by moving away from the centre. To build higher in the

Utilization of shallow harbor for warehouses and railroads. Duluth.

air solves the problem in a banking and office district, but not in a retail shopping district, where ground floor frontage on traffic streets is required. Whether an adjoining lot is acquired or the shopkeeper himself moves, the result is the same, which is the starting of the movement away from the centre, a slow but endless procession. The fact that land is cheaper away from the centre has a slight tendency to further promote the outward movement, which continually evidences the unstable equilibrium between the centripetal force of economy in the transaction of business and the centrifugal force of cheap land. The uniform tendency as a city grows is toward greater concentration in the business centre and greater dispersion in the residence sections, and as long as there is an outward movement so long is there certain to be a continual readjustment at the business centre to conform to it.

The various embryonic sections gathered closely together in the first small area of the city, in expanding largely influence the location

Union Railroad Depot, Toledo. An exceptional case of non-utilization of frontage opposite an important depot due to railroad ownership of land. Many thousands of dollars of income thrown away by not making short-time ground leases.

of utilities. Whatever the new building to be erected, whether retail or wholesale, shop or residence, it can either be placed next to similar buildings or apart from them. With this choice, buildings are usually placed adjacent to others of a similar kind, so that the general tendency for all sections is to extend continuously, expanding in breadth as the centre is left. One expensive residence, if not overcome by unfavorable factors, may be sufficient to attract similar buildings and create the most fashionable residence street in a city, as in a more marked way the royal palaces in Paris and London have created the most fashionable residence districts in those cities.

This, however, does not mean that individual enterprise or whim can run counter to the orderly evolution of a city.

When the best residence district is determined, the main growth of the city is quite certain to follow it, as note the movement of retail stores after the best residences on Fifth Avenue in New York; on Boylston Street in Boston; on Michigan Avenue in Chicago; on Olive and Locust Streets in St. Louis; on Madison, Monroe and Jefferson Streets in Toledo; on Morrison and Washington Streets in Portland, Ore.; on St. Charles, Carondelet and Baronne Streets in New Orleans, etc. The reason the best residence district rather than the largest residence district draws the city is doubtless that

Clark Street, Chicago, in 1857. Showing raised buildings and sidewalks, as city level was altered.

the far higher percentage of purchasing power of the wealthy more than offsets the superior numbers of the poorer classes, and to the further fact that the shops patronized by the wealthy become fashionable, and hence sought by all classes as far as their means permit.

Exceptions to this progression are due chiefly to topography, business remaining on a level if possible and climbing hills only under great pressure. A further exception to the normal would be where two or more good residence districts are located on opposite sides of the main business section so as to balance each other, as in Fort Wayne and Knoxville.

Probably the most important movement within a city as it grows is the gathering together of those carrying on the same kind of business into special districts. This tendency was common in Rome and Constantinople thousands of years ago, and is in harmony with the law of evolution, that increasing differentiation is accompanied by increased integration. Retail stores cluster together at convenient points for their customers and not because they do business with each other. The chief attracting power of such a retail section seems to be the insurance to customers against failure to find within the section what they seek. Undoubtedly the selection within this special district is normally better than that in all the rest of the

Example of absence of influence of public buildings. Post office in Chattanooga, erected twelve years ago, away from business center, has attracted no business.

city combined, and shoppers are saved the time, trouble and uncertainty of seeking through scattered shops. While one shop may attract a customer and another make the sale, such an interchange of customers is probably in the long run closely balanced. The personal factor, or the business ability of managers to advertise and develop a business, is most influential in causing gradations of values in adjacent business locations. A successful shop continually enlarges the area from which it draws custom and diverts special currents of travel towards it. This attracts the notice of other shops in the same line of business, who, reasoning either that the location has helped their successful rival or that by moving near them they can secure some of their customers, move close to the successful store. Formerly it was held that the further a retail store was removed from a competitor the better, but this has been found to hold true only of those small stores which depend for business on the immediate neighborhood.

In many forms of business the clustering together of those transacting it finally crystallizes into an Exchange, which forms the centre

Perry Street, Montgomery, Ala. A curious example of the most fashionable residence street ending abruptly in a meadow, only three blocks from fine houses. Of course axial strength is not necessary for residence streets.

of the district. Since the Exchanges are the result and not the cause of the special districts in which they are located, we must look back of them to find the causes for the location of various utilities. For example, the leather district in New York was located in Beekman Swamp, on account of the wet ground suitable for tanning pits, and similarly in Philadelphia, the leather district was located on both sides of Dock Creek. There were banks on Wall Street long before the Stock Exchange was established, the location of the banks and of the United States Sub-Treasury and Assay Office attracting the Stock Exchange, which in turn drew further Banks, Trust Companies and Brokers. The location of the Cotton Exchange apart from the dry-goods district would seem strange except for the fact that thirty or forty years ago Hanover Square was the centre of the dry-goods trade.

The reasons for the clustering together of wholesale houses are not so clear as in the case of retail shops, except that the features

Cost of excavating high bank has made a break in business buildings on traffic street. First floor of new buildings shown excavated 60 feet back, while upper stories run 120 feet back. First Avenue, Seattle.

which are favorable for one wholesale house are equally so for another, such as proximity to transportation facilities to save trucking, and the fact that by locating together they attract more out-of-town buyers than if scattered.

The outward pressure of one zone upon another involves the slow advance of the banking and office section into the older retail or wholesale districts, the continual following along of the lighter wholesale houses into the buildings vacated by the retail shops, the close pursuit of the best residence sections by the best retail shops, with normally a mixed zone of institutions, etc., acting as a buffer between them, and the steady march of residences into the outlying country, first utilized for gardens or cottages. Whatever the size or shape of a city, the order of dependence of one district upon another remains the same, although many districts are not clearly defined but overlap others of different character.

In connection with the progression of districts in a city, we may note the movement of the point of highest value, which means the

Frontage on traffic street used for advertising purposes. Seattle.

most desirable location for a retail shop in all cities, except in the few financial capitals where the banking and office district produces higher values than retail shops.

In a waterfront city the highest values start at the point of origin and spread normally along the first street on the waterfront, moving later to the next street parallel to it, and so on back.

The rate of this backward growth from street to street varies according to the prosperity of a city, a rapid increase of population being reflected in an expansion of the city's area, and often a rapid shifting of the business centre. In slow growing cities it may take

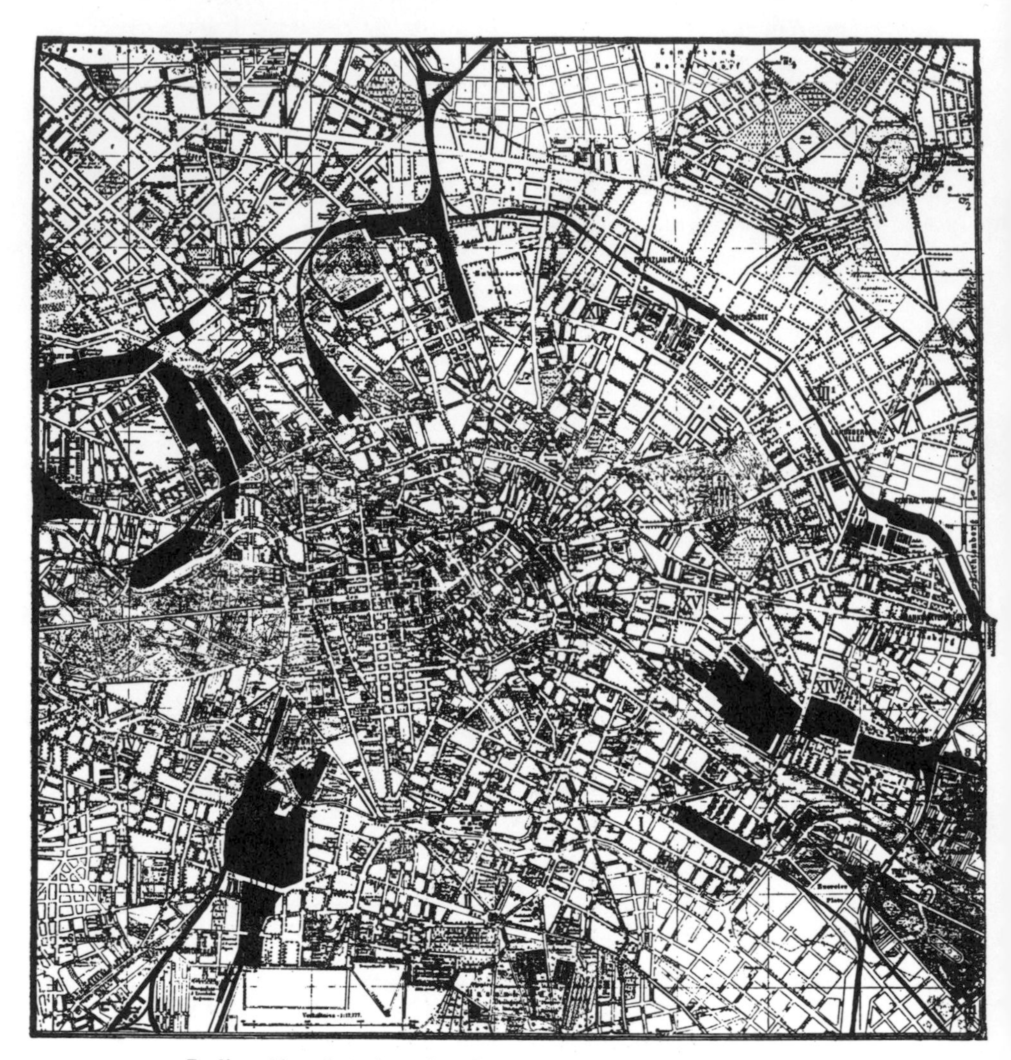

Berlin. The clustering of railroad stations towards the city center illustrates the efforts of railroads, for strategic reasons, to reach the business heart of the city. This map shows only a small part of the city.

from twenty to forty years to move the principal retail business from one street to another, as note the movement from Water Street to Main Street in Bridgeport; from Bay Street to Congress Street and later Broughton Street in Savannah, etc.

If the principal street runs at right angles to the water front, the shifting of the highest point of value takes place much more rapidly than if the street is parallel to the water front, where it has to be moved laterally. The rate instead of averaging from twenty to forty years might vary from eight to twelve years per block, the length of the blocks affecting the movement. One factor delaying such movement would be a strong traffic street at right angles to the principal street, which might hold the highest values at its intersection for many years. Such strong cross streets often produce jumps in the onward movement of the highest values, as with 14th, 23d, 34th and 42d streets in New York.

The rate of movement in cities is sometimes affected by the destruction of whole districts by fire, which brings up the question to owners whether or not to rebuild the same type of buildings on the same locations. In many cases a conflagration causes the erection of handsome new buildings in place of the old ones, so that a new period of higher utility arises. On the other hand, the destruction of individual buildings by fire will have an unfavorable effect if tenants move elsewhere and owners do not rebuild.

The unfolding of a city, with its change in land utilization, shows normally in the case of any lot a slow increase in value up to a high point, after which a gradual decline takes place, with occasional fluctuations varying the main movement. Thus where good residences take the place of small suburban homes, a higher utility supplants the lower, and when these good residences become old-fashioned and are converted into boarding-houses a drop in value will ordinarily occur. This is sometimes offset by the more intense utilization of the land, a larger rent being earned from more people even at lower rates. Moreover, property of this class having the prospect of being overtaken by business buildings has an anticipated value in advance of its yield. When retail stores arrive and become firmly established the high level of value is usually reached, this period lasting possibly thirty to sixty years. As the retail stores move on a lower utility succeeds—and usually a lower value unless the city's increase in population more than offsets the drop in utility—wholesale houses being followed by storage warehouses, cheap tenements, dilapidations, etc., until sometimes land formerly the best in the city becomes so remote from the active business centre as to have little or no value.

CHAPTER VII.

Currents of Travel

THE LIFE of a city involves continual travel, day and night, throughout its entire area, the most notable feature of which, and the basis of its effect on the city's structure, is its regularity. The inhabitants of a city do not intermingle at random, but go from one place to another by the quickest, shortest, or most agreeable route. For example, in New York many thousands of the upper classes have never been west of Sixth Avenue or east of Third Avenue, except to the ferries, and many thousands on the lower east side have never seen Fifth Avenue, while in New Orleans many Creoles have never crossed Canal Street into the American quarter.

The chief daily movements consist of the journeys of business men between their residences and their places of business, the complex interweaving of these men within the business centre and the shorter trips of workmen between their homes and their workshops

In modern cities the main currents of business men's travel are carried by street railroads, so that the travel consists of short trips on foot converging to the street railroads, a long trip in the cars to the business centre and there short trips on foot again. In some cities where there are hills between the business and residence sections, the currents of foot travel follow a zigzag course up and down the hill, it being easier to turn corners than encounter grades. A variation may occur in the return trip where men stop at clubs, cáfes or hotel lobbies, the location of these favorite haunts causing a different route to be taken, with some resulting influence on values.

Within the business districts occur the continual interchange of visits by means of which the business of the city is accomplished. Here, although the trips are short, the necessity for saving time leads to the gathering together of the various forms of business in special districts. In large cities the daily trips of workmen are made chiefly on foot and are widely diffused throughout the tenement districts with small effect except that certain more convenient streets attract cheap shops.

The daily trips of women are made either for shopping, calling or driving. Here, as in men's trips, the travel consists of short trips on foot to the street car lines, which carry the concentrated travel to the largest shops, where the cars are left and the women walk to the other shops. For the same reason of convenience women's shops are crowded together in order to save time in going among them.

The display of goods is vital for shops, and in order to display goods shade is necessary; hence the side of the street which is shady during the part of the day in which women shop is normally worth from 20 per cent. to 40 per cent. and occasionally 100 per cent. more than the sunny side of the street. The west side of streets running north and south, and the south side of streets running east and west, are shady the greater part of the year from about 12 or 1 o'clock on, permitting a display of goods without fear of fading, and rendering the sidewalk agreeable. The greater part of the purchasing in the large shops is done by women of the middle classes, whose household duties prevent them from reaching the shops until after 11 o'clock. The busiest shopping hours are from 11 o'clock to 4 o'clock, many women taking lunch either in the department stores or in restaurants nearby. The women of wealth shop usually in the morning between 11 and 2 o'clock, so that even in their case the west or south side of the street has some advantage of shade. In southern cities, where shade is even more important, the relative value of the four corners of two intersecting business streets is well defined, the southwest corner being the most valuable, the southeast next, the northwest next, and finally the northeast corner. This refers only to retail shopping fronts, the corners having a different order of prefernce if desired for other purposes, such as hotels or office buildings. It is said that in such northern latitudes as those of St. Petersburg and Montreal the sunny side of the street is more valuable than the shady side since it attracts the travel in the long winters. In New York some difference can be noted in the tides of foot travel according to the time of year, but since for eight or nine months of the year the climate is mild, the shops become established on the shady side of the street and whatever travel in winter changes to the sunny side is not sufficient to draw them over.

Other factors are sometimes strong enough to overcome the advantage of shade, such as proximity to a section of customers, as in New York on Sixth Avenue, between 34th and 59th Street, where the east side of the street is more valuable than the west side.

In the larger cities the general use of private carriages by wealthy women influences values, in that the high-grade women's shops seek locations away from car lines and easily accessible to the "carriage trade." Such locations are usually on or near the most fashionable axial streets, such as Fifth Avenue in New York, Michigan Avenue

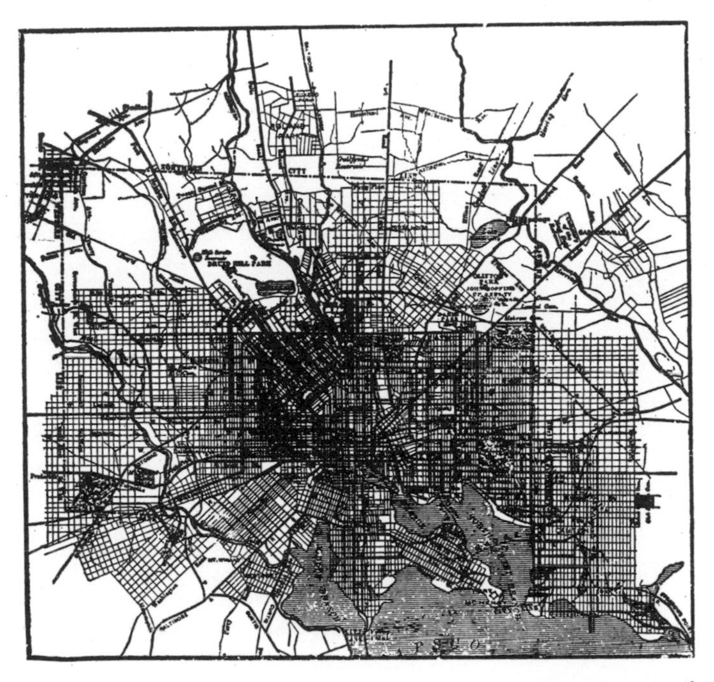

Map of Baltimore, showing street railroad lines, which illustrate the gathering of traffic to the business center and its interchange on intersecting lines.

in Chicago, and Boylston Street in Boston, all of which were fashionable driving streets long before the residences facing them were driven out by shops.

The daily shopping of women clerks, shop girls, etc., is done either at small stores in the neighborhood where they live or at the large department stores, to which they make a special trip, lower prices being more important to them than the time consumed.

The travel of mechanics and laborers in the morning is hurried by their having to report at the workshops at a certain hour, but in the evening they have a chance to shop in the small stores on the way from the factory to their homes. Ordinarily, the time of workmen and their wives is so much occupied during the week that the bulk of their shopping is done on Saturday nights from 6 to 10 o'clock, on the traffic streets which pierce the tenement districts.

In the smaller cities there are so few strangers that their influence may be disregarded. In the large cities there is an important and continuous visiting population, which varies daily as to individuals. The average number of strangers in New York is estimated at 100.000 people, who support many of the theatres, shops, and hotels, the latter being important as the starting points from which the visitors' trips originate.

In the smaller cities suburbanites are few in number, and reaching the business centre chiefly in electric cars merge with the general population and may be disregarded. In the large cities suburbanites arrive by ferry or train and usually make hurried trips to their offices in the morning and back in the evening. This effort to reduce the time between their homes and their business militates against their purchases en route, with the exception of small articles which can be carried, such as fruit, books, flowers, furnishing goods, etc., shops for which locate around some of the ferries and railroad depots. An extreme example of a large current of daily foot travel of the highest económic quality is furnished by the summer travel on Rector Street, New York, where thousands of wealthy men walk daily from the Wall Street section to and from the Sandy Hook boat. Here every factor is favorable to promoting an increase of values, except the speed with which the walking is done and the fact that the traffic lasts only five months of the year, which causes it to have no influence on values.

Added to the daily travel in a city is the evening travel to the theatres, opera, music halls, etc. The theatres, usually on street car lines and near the most important hotels, chiefly attract the evening travel, which in turn draws restaurants, saloons, cigar shops, candy shops, soda water fountains, florist shops, etc. The variations between summer and winter business become more marked the higher the social class, the little shops on the lower east side of New York probably selling an equal amount of goods throughout the year, the shops supplying the wants of the middle classes falling off during the hot summer months, and the season for fashionable shops lasting about five months. The competitors of the fashionable New York shops are the shops at Newport, Lenox, Bar Harbor, and those of Paris and London, and the competitors of the next grade of shops are those of the summer resorts of New Jersey, Long Island, or near New York. Tradesmen in many cases meet this condition by having winter stores in New York and summer stores where their patrons go. In so far as retail purchases are made outside of New York, the earning power and value of retail property in New York is lowered, this varying in proportion to the length of the summer absence.

The main effect of daily currents of travel is on the location of retail stores, increasing traffic being certain ultimately to change any street into a shopping street. As a corollary to this is the important fact that the relocation of the best residence districts is certain to change the axis of the principal travel within the city, which will draw the shops and values to new streets. Such changes of axis have taken place in New York from Pearl Street to Broadway, and from streets parallel to the river front to streets at right angles to it in St. Louis, St. Joseph, Minneapolis, and are now taking place in Toledo, Portland, Ore., and Cincinnati. As shops follow the shifting currents of travel, rentals move with them, the value of retail land depending on the number of people passing, qualified by their purchasing power, the causes which bring them past the property and their method of locomotion. This dependence of retail business on daily traffic is due to the operation of the laws of chance, by which of a given number of passers-by a certain proportion will become customers.

The mention of traffic within a city suggests the double function of a city street as contrasted with the single function of a country road. A country road is a means of communication only, while a city street also furnishes frontage for buildings. Ordinarily, city streets are first a means of communication and later furnish frontage for buildings, but in waterfront cities this may be reversed. The principal business streets usually have some definite point of origin, such as a ferry or a railroad station within a city, or a country town or district outside of it, and long distance or through traffic is a prime essential for business streets, those which are cut off at one or both ends being almost useless for retail business, even though immediately contiguous to main arteries of traffic. Currents of traffic are not always straight, but may follow a street which has turns or angles, or a short street cut through a block between two main business streets, as with New Bond Street in London, and Union Street in Nashville. A serious detriment to values is caused by a break in the continuity of shops, whether due to a vacant lot, a church, a private residence, or an institution of any kind. A row of stores resembles a chain, the insertion of a vacancy or of any different utilization breaking its cohesion.

Besides the main currents of travel, the little feeding streams are closely watched, such shops as hatters, tailors, lunch rooms, men's furnishing goods, etc., locating in the men's district near the office buildings. The grade of shops on the streets leading from the office sections conforms to the character of the passers-by, high-class shops being where employers pass, and cheaper shops where clerks go, while push-carts and hawkers catch the office boy trade.

A noteworthy qualification in the location of retail shops is that the larger and more expensive the articles to be purchased the further people will go in search of them. Large and well managed shops will attract purchasers wherever located, but even such shops are extremely sensitive to the merits of different locations and pay high rents to be exactly where they can obtain the largest number of customers. In all cities there are constant changes in the population, and all shops to be most successful must keep themselves before the public by means of prominent locations.

The most striking feature of the daily travel within a city is its fluidity, or the closeness within which it seeks its own level. Obstructions check it and turn it aside as they would a stream of water. In flowing down a street it backs up each cross street, carrying stores to a distance proportionate to the strength of the current; and where two currents meet the pressure at the intersection intensifies the back currents. The stronger the current the further it spreads back or the greater the depth of shops, in some cases running through the block, as on 23d Street, New York, where the shops extend to 22d Street on one side and 24th Street on the other. Similarly, the stronger the current of traffic the higher it is heaped up, or the taller the buildings to accommodate it. The current of travel, blocked by Washington Square, New York, flowed up Broadway and 6th Avenue and, meeting at 23d Street a back current of business building, has flowed down 5th Avenue, in the same way that a stream meeting a rock divides, the pressure of water causing a current to flow back to the rock.

Street railroads have wrought a revolution in the structure of cities, scattering population over a wide area, adding value to the circumference by rendering it accessible for residences, and to the center by concentrating traffic within it, a part of this added value being removed from the intermediate zone. By rendering new districts accessible, thus increasing the area of supply of land, the value of all competitive land is reduced, so that the effect of street railroads on residence land is to lower its average value. The speed of an electric car is so great that the tendency is not to add on gradually to existing residence sections, but to project beyond them into the cheap country land. Ordinarily, capitalistic handling takes hold of a new outlying district and, by laying out fine streets and sidewalks, sewers, water, gas, electric light, etc., and erecting high-class houses, establishes a residence section of higher values than much of the residence land nearer the business center. Opposed to this condition are the two factors of long settlement, which makes old residents reluctant to move, and the cost of car fares, amounting to between $5 and $10 per month according to the size of the family, which operate in favor of the old-fashioned residence sections near the business center.

It may happen that the best business street in a city has no car line on it, as for example Nicollet Avenue in Minneapolis; 6th Street in St. Paul, and Felix Street in St. Joseph, these being for this reason better adapted to the "carriage trade." An example of the effect of street railroads on carriage trade occurred in New York when the construction of the electric roads on Broadway and 23d Street produced such a dangerous intersection that ladies were timid about driving across it. This hastened the northward movement of high-class shops from Broadway below 23d Street to 5th Avenue above 25th Street.

Transfer points, owing to concentration of daily streams of people and consequent opportunity for shops, are strategic points in a city's area, creating business sub-centers, whose prospects of increasing values are limited only by the number and quality of the people likely to utilize them. As examples, note the marked effect of transfers in New York at Broadway and 34th Street, Madison Avenue and 59th Street, Lexington Avenue and 59th Street; also in New Haven at Chapel and Church Streets; in Denver at 15th and Lawrence Streets, and the many transfer points in the outlying districts of Chicago.

The success of street railroads in running cars to the top of fairly high hills has added millions of dollars of value to the higher lands in all hilly cities, as in San Francisco, Seattle, Peoria, etc.

Similarly, every improvement in the construction, operation or service of street railroads strengthens their influence on the structure of cities. In general, if a city has less than the normal street railroad mileage the result is a number of small business sub-centers in outlying districts, and a consequent irregular diffusion of values, while a well developed street railroad system renders stable the normal distribution of values.

In the largest cities the elevated railroads have the same general effects as the electric street railroads, with the additional influence of removing value from between the stations and increasing it at the stations. Despite the heavy damages paid by the elevated roads in New York, it is doubtful if they have injured many properties. It is certainly noteworthy that over 50 per cent. of the property owners affected did not claim damages from the elevated roads, also that the regular scale of damages paid out of court is only $10 per front foot. One beneficial result of the elevated road between stations is in affording shopkeepers along the route an opportunity to display advertising signs and goods on the upper floors. Where the elevated stations are only five blocks apart, as on the 6th Avenue line in the shopping district from 14th to 23d Streets, no building being more than 600 feet from an elevated station, the crowds from the different stations intermingle, so that all stores on the short stretches between the stations are benefited by the travel.

Where stations are ten blocks apart there is no such overlapping of streams of travel, but if there were sufficient travel to demand it there would be additional stations, in which case the beneficial effects of the elevated would be intensified and the detrimental effects diminished, so that it might be said to be the fault of the property that it has not sufficient business strength to make an elevated road a source of additional value rather than the reverse. While an elevated road is always detrimental in a residence section, and partly detrimental and partly helpful in a small business section, in the most patronized retail shopping sections it is a strong advantage.

The influence of an underground road is similar to that of the elevated, except that the feature of advertising is absent. The longer haul of an underground road creates residence values at still greater distances, and also still further intensifies values at the center of the city and at all stations, especially express stations.

Bridges, ferries and tunnels, which serve as additional outlets to a city, co-operate with long distance transportation facilities, and any change in their location or any competition of new bridges or tunnels by changing traffic routes cause marked shifting of values. Thus the construction of the Brooklyn Bridge by diverting traffic from the old Fulton Street ferry, and throwing it half a mile back from the river on either side, removed millions of dollars of value from the streets leading to the ferries, especially in Brooklyn.

CHAPTER VIII.

Types of Buildings

LET US consider next the types of buildings erected for different utilities and their reflex effects on values. The most important consideration governing suitability to location is that of proportion of cost of building to value of land, the safe general rule being that the cost of the building should approximately equal the value of the land. In other words, the typical successful property, land and building, appears to earn double interest on the cost of the building, one-half of which capitalized as economic rent gives a value to the land equal to the cost of the building. While there are exceptions to this proportion it forms a median line of departure, applying most closely to business property, whether the building is a $5,000 one-story brick on a cheap lot or a $3,000,000 office building in the highest priced location. The chief destruction of capital comes from the erection of expensive buildings on cheap lots, while the erection of cheap buildings, known as tax payers, even on expensive land, should not lead to loss, although it may not lead to great profit. On a street whose traffic is increasing rapidly a business building costing several times the value of the land may profitably be erected, since within ten years the value of the land may overtake the cost of the building. If, however, the building runs at a low return for ten years the investment may prove a poor one, and the compromise of erecting one or two stories of sufficient strength to carry later five or six is sometimes the best solution.

In the largest cities increasing demand for space in favored localities has steadily increased the height of buildings, the practical checks arising from time to time having been successively overcome by new inventions. While fifty years ago the average height of business buildings in New York was three or four stories, and in the best locations five or six stories, the general use of elevators after 1870 ran the height up to eight or nine stories, where it was checked by the expense of the heavy walls and by the waste of the most

The economic error here consists of placing ornamental columns in front of the offices on either side of the entrance—especially the column on each end—causing vacancies and low rents, representing an average loss of probably 4 per cent. on $200,000. The entrance to a large and important building should be duly emphasized, but such sacrifice of income is unnecessary. Broadway and Leonard Street, New York.

valuable space on the ground floor taken up by the walls. Skeleton steel construction, developed since 1890, has saved the space on the ground floor, modified the cost of the highest buildings and run them up to twelve or sixteen stories, which express elevators have lifted to twenty-five and thirty stories.

When skyscrapers were first erected it was the common opinion that buildings of this character in the midst of low buildings, by cutting off their light and air robbed them of their rights, so that justice demanded a legal limit to the height of buildings. It was soon found out, however, that where a skyscraper was so built as to require light and air from the adjoining lot, it was the owner of the small lot who had the skyscraper at his mercy. The threat of

Chamber of Commerce, Duluth. Badly planned front; over 60% of frontage wasted on stone masonry and entrances, leaving less than 40% to earn ground floor rentals. Building has been financially unsuccessful.

replacing the low building with a high one, destroying the value of possibly a quarter to a third of the skyscraper, has quite uniformly compelled the owner of the skyscraper to buy or lease for a long term of years the adjoining property, as with the American Surety Building, Washington Life Building, etc. Skyscrapers being naturally located on corners, the typical development of a small block would consist of four high buildings on the four corners and four low ones between them controlled by the high ones. With long, narrow blocks, as in New York, the development would be more irregular, the tendency being to alternate high and low buildings Further variations occur where a skyscraper owns one or two lots in an adjoining tract in order to block the erection of another high

Chamber of Commerce, Cincinnati; designed by H. H. Richardson. A magnificent building, but with income from ground floor subordinated to the architectural design.

building, as with the Park Row Realty Building, and the Broad Exchange Building, or the purchase of low buildings across narrow streets to insure light and air, as with some of the life insurance company buildings.

The height of buildings has been limited by statute in Boston and Chicago, and attempts have been made to do so in New York, but the general sentiment seems to be that the economic check is sufficient.

When skyscrapers were new, rents diminished from the ground floor up, as in older buildings, but, the upper stories being more desirable on account of better light and air and freedom from noise and dust, the rents were soon equalized. The demand for the upper stories has continued, so that in some buildings higher rents are charged for them, the least desirable floors being from the third to the sixth, this less productive stratum furnishing an economic check to the height of buildings.

Wherever modern office buildings have been erected, the advantages they offer have drawn tenants from the dark and old-fashioned buildings surrounding them. The offset to owners from this destruction of capital in old buildings by modern improvements is the increase in the value of the land due to the possibility of similarly

Planned for a bank building. The solid wall of stone and brick ten feet high throws away the ground floor frontage, from which the chief income should be obtained. Berlin Building, Tacoma.

improving their land. Old property two or three blocks away, however, may lose its tenants without any corresponding gain in values, since the increase in space supplied by the skyscraper is so great that its district is more limited. As illustrating the increase of floor space from high buildings, the Bowling Green Building increased the floor space on the same area from 80,000 to 567,000 square feet, and the German-American Building from 26,000 to 126,000 square feet. An example of a shrinking office district was offered by lower Wall Street, where of late years buildings have been vacant owing to the completion of the new buildings around the banking center at the intersection of Wall and Nassau Streets. As the office district spreads the old locations regain value, and lower Wall Street is now building up with skyscrapers. Similarly the old three- and four-story buildings on lower Broadway became unremunerative and some were closed up, until the Bowling Green Building with its modern facilities attracted tenants. The concentration of the office district caused by skyscrapers results in a great saving of time in the interchange of business, and hence an economic gain to the community.

Subject to limitations from changing conditions and local circumstances in different cities, the following table is an estimate of the character of business buildings, as to cost, height and material, which may suitably be erected on land of varying values:

On land valued per front foot.	Buildings may cost per cubic foot about:	Construction of buildings may be:	Height of buildings may be:
$200	8 to 10 cents	Ordinary brick	2 story
300	8 " 10 "	Ordinary brick	3 "
500	8 " 10 "	Ordinary brick	3 to 4 "
800	12 " 20 "	Ordinary brick	4 " 5 "
1,000	12 " 20 "	Slow-burning	5 " 6 "
1,500	12 " 20 "	Slow-burning	5 " 6 "
2,000	18 " 25 "	Tending to fireproof	7 " 9 "
3,000	18 " 25 "	Tending to fireproof	7 " 9 "
6,000	30 " 50 "	Skeleton steel, fireproof	10 " 12 "
15,000	30 " 50 "	Skeleton steel, fireproof	12 " 20 "
18,000—35,000	30 " 50 "	Skeleton steel, fireproof	20 " 30 "

Turning to residences, the proportion of cost of building may vary from one and a half to three times the value of the land, except as to workmen cottages, where it may vary from three to five times the value of the land. The highest grade houses are ordinarily built for homes and cost more than they will sell for or than their rentals will pay interest on, this lack of commercial value increasing with the cost of the house. In expensive houses in smaller cities there is a tendency towards restoring the equilibrium between the value of the land and buildings by placing them on plots of 100 to 150 feet front by 200 to 400 feet deep. This equilibrium is more apparent than real, since not over 75 feet of frontage is necessary for the house, the balance of the land being a luxury on which taxes are paid and interest lost. In all cases the cost of the house should be closely proportioned to the cost of the surrounding houses—a $50,000 house in the midst of $5,000 houses, or a $5,000 house in the midst of $1,000 houses having a commercial value but little in excess of the cheaper neighboring houses. Instances could be cited of houses costing five times as much as the surrounding houses which have not sold for as much as the cheaper ones, because rich people will not live among cheap houses and poor people cannot afford to keep up large houses. Such houses usually sell for boarding-houses or sanitoriums. On the other hand, a small house in the midst of expensive ones will usually sell and rent well, there being strong competition to obtain a residence location of social importance at small outlay. There is, however, a limit to the erection of cheap residences in good locations, a large number of them spoiling the value of locations otherwise suitable for handsome residences, and some houses in fashionable sections being too small to sell well.

The error consists in placing entrance to three-story building on principal street instead of side street. These 16 feet would have yielded from $1,500 to $2,500 per annum for the past ten years, or 6% on $25,000 to $40,000. The error has been partly remedied by blocking the entrance with a cigar stand, yielding $720 per annum. Second and Cherry Streets, Seattle.

Turning to the larger cities, houses built in blocks represent a pressure of population on land which does not permit the use of land for light and air around detached houses. In this class of residences the cost of the house should not greatly exceed the value of the land, with a general tendency, where the land is cheap, of the cost of the houses exceeding the land value, and where the land is expensive, the cost of the houses being less than the land value. A

Front of corner store in Duluth. About as badly planned as possible.

still more intense pressure of population on land results in apartment houses, which may properly vary in cost from two to four times the value of the land. Where apartment houses are built in smaller cities, especially if they are large and expensive, they anticipate a pressure on land which has not yet arrived, and are apt to be unsuccessful. Such apartment houses sometimes cost ten to fifteen times the value of the land, the danger of such a top-heavy investment being the abundance of competing land which can be cheaply obtained, and the fact that almost the entire investment is in the building, which is certain to depreciate physically. For example, where a $50,000 apartment house has been erected on $5,000 of land, assuming in 10 years a 30% depreciation of the building, or $15,000, and a 30% appreciation of the land, or $1,500, the net capital loss would be $13,500. The mistake of all owners who erect expensive buildings on cheap land is in not realizing that buildings erected to rent do not

Income from corner about 50% of what it should be, due to error of architect, who aimed at a massive appearance. Morrison and Sixth Streets, Portland, Ore.

dominate their environment. The advantage of an even division of investment between land and building is clear, in that as against the certain physical depreciation of the building there may be an appreciation of the land to offset it. Where tall apartment houses are erected on the corners of the traffic streets they injure the value of the adjacent lots on the side streets, despite their acting as buffers to the noise and dust of the traffic streets.

With limitations, the following is an estimate of the character of residences as to cost, size and construction, which may suitably be erected on land of varying values:

On land valued per front ft.	Av'ge frontage of lot.	Construction may be	Residences may cost: Per cu. ft. cents	Total	
$5 in smaller cities	25	Frame detached ..	5 to 7	$400 to	$800
10 " " "	25	" " ...	5 " 7	800 "	1,000
20 " " "	30	" " ...	5 " 8	1,500 "	2,000
30 " " "	40	" or brick ...	6 " 9	2,500 "	3,000
40 " " "	40	" " ...	7 " 10	3,000 "	4,000
50 " " "	50	Brick detached....	8 " 12	4,500 "	6,000
75 " " "	60	" or stone "	10 " 15	6,000 "	10,000
100 " " "	60—100	" " " "	12 " 18	10,000 "	20,000
150 " " "	60—100	" " " "	15 " 20	12,000 "	30,000
250 " " "	75—150	" " " "	15 " 25	15,000 "	50,000
500 " largest "	12—16	Brick or stone block	10 " 15	6,000 "	15,000
750 " " "	16—20	" " " "	12 " 18	10,000 "	20,000
1,000 " " "	20—25	" " " "	15 " 20	20,000 "	50,000
2,000 " " "	20—30	" " " "	18 " 25	40,000 "	60,000
3,000 " " "	25—40	Fireproof	30 up.	100,000 "	150,000
5,000 " " "	30—50	"	40 "	200,000 "	400,000
7,500—9,000" "	40—100	"	50 "	500,000 up.	

One feature affecting the suitability of buildings to land is that of the life of buildings. The useful life of a building may be ended

Equally massive, but steps omitted. Rents sacrificed. The dealer in sewing machines and bicycles can only exhibit six bottles of oil in each window to attract customers. Morrison and Seventh Straeets, Portland, Ore.

from any one of four causes: Physical decay, destruction by fire, change of utility, or competition of new buildings.

The physical decay of ordinary buildings depends more on repairs than on the character of the original materials used. Steel frame buildings are of such recent invention that their life has not yet been tested, but engineers estimate that they will last several hundred years.

An estimate of the physical depreciation of buildings if kept in repair would be as follows:

Class of building	Life in years.	Annual depreciation.
Cheap frame tenements	10 to 15	5 to 10%
Ordinary frame residences	25 " 30	2 " 3%
Cheap brick tenements and office buildings	25 " 30	2 " 3%
Cheap brick or stone residences	35 " 50	1 " 2%
Better class frame residences	35 " 50	1 " 2%
" " brick and stone residences	50 " 75	1 " 1½%
Good brick and stone office buildings	75 " 100	1%
Steel skeleton buildings	Unknown	...

The loss from a change of utility is modified by the greater or less convertibility of business buildings, many office buildings being convertible into hotels or lodgings. Thus the old Astor House was changed into an office building twenty or thirty years ago, but was reconverted into a hotel, and there are many instances in western cities of buildings used interconvertibly for lodgings or offices. The destruction of buildings from change of utility constitutes an offset to increased value in land, in that the more rapid the increase in land value, the more rapid the destruction of value in the building. In locations of rapidly changing utility, old buildings are generally considered to be of no value. The correct basis of their value, however, would be the amount of gross rents they will earn before being removed, less such expenses as are due to their still standing, such as insurance, repairs, taxes on the building only, etc. From this standpoint the great number of old buildings are generally undervalued, since the process of replacing them is certain to be a gradual one.

Competition of new buildings operates more strongly in the case of residences and office buildings than of retail shopping buildings. As to residences, for example, when the public has been educated to prefer light stone or brick renaissance houses to the old-fashioned brownstone front, and modern interior arrangements, decoration and plumbing to former styles and equipment, the value of the old house has about departed, even though it is in good physical condition. As to shops, the location is paramount, and tenants pay high rents for the ground floor with little regard to the architectural appearance of the building above.

The natural tendency to erect continually better and handsomer buildings is an added force drawing retail shops onward into new locations. Thus, while the best business street in an old city has

Type of blocked entrance with more than 50% of frontage taken up by obstructions. Royal Street, Mobile.

usually been built up with brick houses two or three stories high and converted into shops on the ground floor, the buildings on the next business street are larger and better built, and so on until the best section is reached. Sometimes the best buildings when new are rented for less than the old ones, but as tenants are attracted the pressure of demand causes rents to advance in the new buildings, while removals cause rents to drop in the old ones. When the rents in the new buildings are the highest in the city the shifting of the shop centre and point of highest value has been accomplished. Efforts are sometimes made to bring back tenants to the old buildings by improving them, but rarely succeed, because the onward movement

A repelling approach to a store. Liberty Street, near William Street, New York.

is too strong to be overcome and because the efforts are usually made too late and without co-operation among the owners of the declining street. The owners of property yielding the highest rents in the city usually anticipate nothing but continued increase of rents and seldom realize that the business centre of a city can shift until declining rents bring this fact forcibly to their attention. Even then many of them have not the courage or enterprise to tear down their old buildings and erect handsome new ones, and others are financially unable to do so, it being more difficult to obtain building loans on a declining street than on an improving street.

How to carry on business behind a granite quarry is the problem confronting the prospective tenant. A common error of architects is to sacrifice income from store frontage to "solidity" of construction. Jersey Central Building, Liberty and Washington Streets, New York.

To take up the general effects of the erection of buildings, these may either increase, diminish or have no effect upon the value of the land covered and the surrounding land. The hypothesis of absence of effect may be eliminated, since while the selling price of a lot may not be affected, some effect on the surroundings will surely result. The first principle is that if the building is suited to the needs of the location and is equal to or superior in construction, arrangement and appearance to existing buildings, it tends to increase values, while if inferior and cheaper than existing buildings it tends to depress them. Such an effect of inferior buildings is by no means uniform, as there are locations in which the erection of any building, however poor, increases values.

The effects of buildings differ chiefly according to whether they are erected in a built-up section within a city or in new territory on its outskirts. If erected in a built-up section, old buildings are removed to make place for the new ones, public attention is attracted to the locality and the prices of surrounding land stiffen. The new buildings are quite certain to draw some tenants from the older surrounding buildings, so that their rents and value will diminish, while the land being suitable for better buildings will increase in value.

Corner store on Nicollet Avenue, Minneapolis. Removing brick work to permit more show windows. A not uncommon reconstruction.

The building of new residences in long-established residence sections tends to increase values, public opinion being apt to concede a new lease of life for possibly thirty or forty years to the old residence district.

When buildings are erected on the outskirts of a city where the conversion from agricultural land to building land is taking place, the character of the buildings will at first determine the value of the land. Such districts afford highly competitive sites, where the only difference between lots, barring topography, is in transportation facilities, so that building operators can control values in the new territory by their scale of development, as in South Brooklyn. This is always assuming that the speculative buildings shall be utilized at a normal return on the capital invested, which is begging the whole question. It is the business of building operators to know what class of people can be attracted to the new areas, and their success or failure in moving population to occupy the new houses, and in attracting various classes of people, determines the scale of values. From the standpoint that land has no value until there is demand for its utilization, there is a theoretical gain in transforming speculative or anticipated value into actual value, but the future of all outlying land

Good and bad store fronts. The store on street level with good windows yields about 25% more rent than the adjoining one. Madison Street, Toledo.

is discounted many years ahead, so that prices may drop after development. The worst that can happen to a suburban tract is that it should be forced on the market before there is a demand for it, the result being that poor people attracted by low prices will build cheap houses there and create a shabby and repulsive district, which, if large enough, may act as a bar to the city's growth in that direction. There are many cases, of course, where such occupancy is but temporary, as with the shanty settlements on the upper west side in New York, and the negro ownership on residence streets in Washington.

Whether within or without a city, much can be done to force value into land by the erection of handsome buildings, if done on a large scale. It is true that tenants seeking accommodations are com-

The five-foot strip on the corner, yielding a large income for a saloon and advertising, illustrates the high value of a good location, even though the area is small. Broadway, New York.

pelled to take them where they exist, except that if good tenants want buildings erected on new sites they can always secure them, capital being easily found where income is assured. This vital limitation to a hypothetical monopoly of existing buildings demonstrates again the fact that it is effective demand and not buildings which creates values.

The building which is most suitable to its location may be defined as that one which will for the longest term of years yield the largest and most certain net return. The time element in this definition eliminates such buildings as a factory in a residence district, or a saloon in a business location, which while yielding a large rent injures the surrounding property. There are cases in rapidly changing sections where the most suitable building is one some years in advance of the time, since the utility of the building yielding the highest present rent will in a few years disappear, necessitating its destruction or reconstruction. Many such cases of discounting the future, though carefully reasoned, have resulted unsuccessfully, owing either to the direction of growth or, equally important, the rate of growth, being

Good planning of light well used for stores. Augusta, Ga.

misjudged. The community feels its way along a few buildings at a time in one direction or another, watching carefully where anticipated demand is not realized and unsuccessful buildings point a warning. The main principle seems to be that the best neighbors any building can have are buildings similar to itself, business buildings and residences being most keenly responsive to environment, and public buildings, factories, churches, hospitals, transportation terminals, etc., being more independent.

Before outlining the normal yield and resulting land values of the various utilities, we may note that the chief variation in them is in the form of deductions due to nuisances, under which name we may class anything tending to depreciate the value of land. The character of nuisances varies according to the section in which they are located, the cheaper the property the more impregnable to attack, and the more expensive the property the more sensitive to the levelling power of proximity, the tendency of all adjoining buildings being to strike a mean.

To classify nuisances, those affecting retail business property are adjoining vacancies, whether caused by rebuilding, fire, removals or

Good store front. Wide and low windows. Piers covered by showcases. Summit Street, Toledo.

failures, low class neighbors such as saloons, dilapidations, whether of buildings, sidewalks or surroundings, and topographical faults, such as sharp variations of grade, underground streams or quick sands. One of the most serious drawbacks which could happen to business buildings would be the construction of a viaduct carrying all the traffic past them at an elevation, as with the 8th Street viaduct in Kansas City and the High Holborn Viaduct in London, the latter being constructed to avoid the blocking of traffic at the intersection of Oxford and Farringdon's Streets. In office sections the chief nuisance to tall buildings consists of their being crowded so close together as to cut off light and air from each other. Apart from this, skyscrapers remote from the earth's surface have but little to fear, unless it be the chimney of adjoining lower buildings, which can be compelled to run up higher if the smoke is objectionable. Temporary nuisances, however, may arise at the ground level, such as streets torn up for repairs, the laying of pipes, etc., or sidewalks blocked while an adjacent building is being erected.

Good store front. Great width between piers. Low show windows with prism glass above. Summit Street, Toledo.

Residences are more easily affected than business property, although values are lower, in that the erection of almost any building other than a residence constitutes a nuisance. For example, all kinds of factories, even those which emit neither smell nor noise; power-houses of street railroads; hospitals, largely for fear of infection; public schools, on account of the noise made by the scholars; business buildings, hotels or apartment houses, on account of their taking away light, air and quiet from the adjoining property; low lands, owing to fear of malaria—and all cheap, old and dilapidated buildings constitute nuisances. All rough and rocky land, or a steep grade with bluffs, hollows, standing pools or ponds, is undesirable, unless the unsightliness has been taken away by conversion into small parks. Stables constitute the most common nuisance to residences in New York, a "stable street" having a greatly diminished value, as for example, lots on 55th Street, west of 5th Avenue, sold

Recessed front with piers utilized for show cases. A good plan for so narrow a street as Nassau Street, New York.

for about half the price of those on 54th Street, and lots on 52d Street, east of 5th Avenue, about two-thirds the price of those on 51st Street. Street railroads, which in the smaller cities may raise residence values, in the larger cities are always nuisances on residence streets, one certain result being that they attract shops, and when this process begins the desirability of the street for residence ends.

An elevated railroad renders any street through which it runs impossible for residences, while steam railroads ordinarily drive residences a block or two away. Where a railroad runs in part or in

Example of converted building. Old style residence altered into stores. Denver.

First Presbyterian Church located back from street. With growth of retail business on Fourth Street the space in front was built in with stores and offices. Entrance to church through building shown by sign. Cincinnati.

whole through a tunnel, as with the New York Central above 56th Street, the injurious effect is modified.

Even residences are a nuisance to their neighbors if they occupy an abnormal proportion of their lot area, as where the entire lot is covered except for a side light well.

So many and so severe are the nuisances to residence property that many residence neighborhoods are controlled by restrictions, usually running with the land, but sometimes limited in time. In the smaller cities the ordinary restrictions in new residence sections

provide that the premises shall be occupied for residence purposes exclusively, that no residence shall be erected costing less than a given amount, and that no residence shall be placed within a certain distance of the front line of the lots. Such restrictions greatly enhance values, in guaranteeing protection against cheap buildings, stores, saloons, etc. In New York the Murray Hill restriction to residences is well known, this having undoubtedly helped to keep stores and apartments away from some locations on Murray Hill. As instancing the value of a restriction, recently on 53d Street, west of Fifth Avenue, the owner of the only two lots not restricted to private residences, having planned an apartment house, was paid $25,000 to restrict them to private residences. The chief disad-

Change of utilization of building. Church converted into a stable. Cheap location, not suitable for retail business. Minneapolis.

vantage in restricting land to certain uses is that the utility of American city land changes rapidly, and when residence property should be converted to stores but cannot owing to restrictions, a serious detriment to values occurs.

CHAPTER IX.

Rentals and Capitalization Rates

While gross rents are fixed by competition, the question arises how do bidders determine what they can pay? The basis differs radically between business property which earns income for the occupant as well as the owner, and residence property, which for the occupant consumes income only.

Example of misplaced **building.** Expensive building on cheap land. Foreclosed and sold at heavy loss. East Portland, Ore.

The gross rents of business property are gauged from the eonomic standpoint, these being in the long run the normal proportion of what the property can earn for the tenant. The proportion of gross receipts which a shopkeeper pays as rent varies according to his ability as a tradesman, the character and class of his business, and the location, a fair average being from 20% to 40%. The better the location for retail trade the higher the proportion of receipts paid for rent. For retail trade the location and the consequent advertising perform the vital function of selling the goods, and the shopkeeper can largely devote his energies to selecting what the people want.

No. 1. Contrast of income between extravagant and cheap buildings. This building, which cost $396,000, has always yielded, in good times and bad, less net income than the building across the street, which cost under $20.000. This due both to bad planning of expensive building and to high ratio of expenses. 50% to 60% versus 15% for the cheap buildings. Second and Cherry Streets, Seattle. (See following picture.)

Similarly, though in a less marked way, prominent office buildings help to advertise the business of their tenants. On the other hand, mercantile property not on traffic streets, wholesalers, etc., pay but a small proportion of their receipts as rent, the saving, however, going to the hire of drummers to sell goods.

The gross rents of residences represent the proportion of income which various classes can afford to pay for house rent. While the return for such expenditure is chiefly the satisfaction of suitable surroundings, social ambition influences all classes to live in the best neighborhoods within their reach. The proportion of rent to income varies from 15% or 20% among the wealthy, up to 25% or 35% among tenement dwellers. Taking as gross rents the amounts actually received and not the full rental value, from which an allowance for vacancies must be made, we may note first the great difference in the proportion of operating expenses according to the class of property, this varying from 10% for one- or two-story brick store buildings, up to 50% for office buildings or apartment houses.

Explaining this difference is the fact that in office buildings and

No 2. Contrast of income between extravagant and cheap buildings. These cheap buildings opposite expensive building shown in previous picture.

	Cheap buildings.	Expensive buildings
Gross rents	$ 19,600	$ 34,000
Expenses	2,900	18,200
Net rents	$ 16,700	$ 15,800
Or 6% on	278,000	263,000
Deduct building	20,000	396,000
Property earns 6% net on	$258,000	minus $133,000

In other words, the expensive building is capital wasted.

apartment houses from 20% to 25% of the rent represents the payment for services, such as light, heat, elevator, janitors, cleaning, etc. If from gross rentals all service charges are deducted, the other charges, taxes, insurance, repairs and rent collecting, approximate in percentage quite closely in all classes of property.

Example of misplaced building. In the depression of 1893-1898 this building did not quite pay expenses, leaving no return for the land, which cost $100,000, or for the building, which cost $240,000, while adjoining one and three-story buildings on less valuable land, covering same area, paid 6% net on value of building, and $600 per front foot for the land. The error consisted in placing bank and office building in small retail section. Yester Way, Seattle.

Average taxes vary somewhat in different cities. Taxes on individual properties in the same city vary more sharply owing to irregular assessing by tax officials. Figuring the average of a large number of American cities, taxes range from 1¼% to 1½% of actual value, the chief exceptions being in Washington, where taxes amount to 6-10% (the U. S. Government paying half the taxes), and in San Francisco, where taxes amount to 8-10% (the city having no bonded debt). The chief errors of assessors come from their over-estimate of external appearances and from the habit of following former assessment rolls, so that quite uniformly property which has been valuable but which is deteriorating is assessed higher than property in the line of growth and yielding larger rents.

Example of misplaced building. Expensive eleven-story fireproof office building placed about 150 feet off the principal street. Has earned from 2% to 3% net per annum as against a probable 5% if on the best street. Land 60 feet by 62 feet, appraised $25,500, or $425 per front foot for half depth. Building, $160,000. Building costs 6½ times the land, a "top-heavy" investment. Columbus, Ohio.

The cost of insurance is usually so slight that it can be disregarded in making up the budget of annual expenses. Rates range from 15c. to 30c. per $100 per annum for first-class risks in the larger cities, 50c. to 75c. per $100 on first-class risks in the smaller cities, $1.00

per $100 on stores and office buildings in the smaller cities, and so on up.

Leases vary in their provisions as to payment for repairs by landlord and tenant, but if paid by the tenant the rent is proportionately reduced. Average repairs vary from one-half of 1% of the value of the building per annum in the case of the highest type of fireproof buildings, 1% for ordinary mercantile buildings, 2%

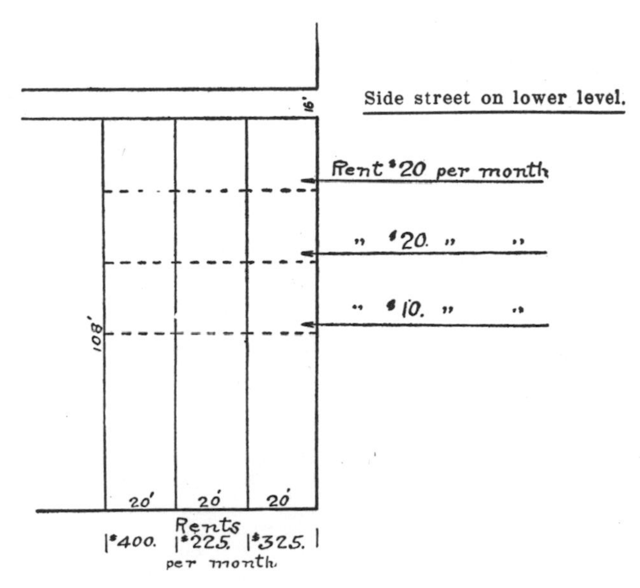

Rentals on traffic street $11,400 versus $600 on side street, or nearly 20 to 1. This illustrates the severe drop in rentals and values off from a traffic street. (In the present instance partly due to grade on side street.) Corner Second and Marion Streets, Seattle.

for older property or that of cheaper construction, 3% to 4% for old tenements, and so on up in proportion to the age, character of construction, and lack of care of the buildings.

The cost of rent collecting averages from 2½% to 3% of the rent receipts in the larger cities, according to the class of property, and about 5% in the smaller cities, according to the class of property. Owners who are competent to manage real estate may save agents' commissions by so doing, but instances are not uncommon, especially as to large business property, where owners managing their own property lose their time and from 20% to 30% of the income which an expert rental agent could have obtained.

An estimated scale of proportion of total operating expenses and net rents would be as follows, the cost of services where rendered, as in office buildings, apartments and some tenements, being included in expenses:

	Expenses.	Net rents.
Low retail or wholesale buildings..............	10-25%	90-75%
Residences	20-30%	80-70%
Non-elevator office buildings	25-35%	75-65%
Tenements, non-elevator and elevator..........	25-45%	75-55%
Elevator apartments	40-55%	60-45%
Fireproof office buildings	40-55%	60-45%

Example of expensive residence wrongly located in suburbs of Indianapolis. Later surrounded by cheap cottages. Land and building appraised at $48,000. Mortgaged for $20,000. Foreclosed and sold ten years later for $1,900.

It is clear that the lower the cost of the building in proportion to the value of the land, the nearer the income approaches to pure ground rent, against which the sole charge is taxes. On the other hand, the more expensive the building the higher the maintenance cost, owing both to the greater number of services rendered and to the higher standard of accommodation. Since the operating expenses of a building, whether fully or only partly occupied, vary but slightly, the larger the proportion of expenses to gross rentals the more marked will be the rise or fall of net rentals as gross rentals fluctuate. Ordinarily, expensive office buildings are properly located, the chief errors being in the erection of expensive buildings in small cities, or in poor locations in larger cities. When hard times cause a sharp drop in rents in the smaller cities, instances have been known of the upper floors of such buildings not earning sufficient rent to pay for the mere services rendered, so that it would pay for owners to close the buildings above the ground floor, even though the ground floor stores are in active demand. The danger to owners of heavy fixed charges is shown in the following table:

With percentage of expenses to gross inc.:	If gross rents rise or fall	Then net rents rise or fall	If gross rents rise or fall	Then net rents rise or fall	If gross rents rise or fall	Then net rents rise or fall
10%	20%	22%	40%	44%	60%	66%
20%	20%	25%	40%	50%	60%	75%
30%	20%	29%	40%	56%	60%	85%
40%	20%	33%	40%	66%	60%	100%
50%	20%	40%	40%	80%	60%	120%
60%	20%	50%	40%	100%	60%	150%

The next charge against gross rents is for interest on capital invested in the building, this being figured at the same rate as the capitalization of the ground rent, after an allowance for depreciation has been made.

The final residuum constitutes the economic or ground rent, which represents the competitive premium paid for location. Where there is no residuum of ground rent in city land it does not follow that the land has no value, but usually that the improvements are not suitable, so that the value must be estimated under a different utilization. If the improvement is a suitable one, absence of ground rent may be due to temporary drop in rentals or bad management, all city land normally yielding some ground rent.

With an established economic rent, the sole remaining factor to transform this into intrisic value is the rate of capitalization. As capitalization rates vary with securities, Government bonds selling below a 2% basis, railroad bonds and stocks on a 3½% to 5% basis, and industrials on a 7% to 10% basis, so the rates of capitalization of urban rents vary from 4% for the highest-class property in the largest cities to 5% and 6% for second-class property in the same cities, or for first-class property in smaller cities; 7%, 8% and 10% for tenements in the largest cities, and 12% to 15% for temporary utilizations or disreputable purposes in the smaller cities. The great power of capitalization rates on values is due to the fact that for every change of 1% in the rate of capitalization values may change from twelve to twenty-five times the difference in interest. For

Substantial buildings from which rentals and value have departed. Land and building would sell for less than half the cost of the building. Front Street, Portland, Ore.

example, a property with a net income of $10,000 would sell on an 8% basis at $125,000, on a 6% basis at $166,000, and on a 4% basis at $250,000. The lower the capitalization rate the greater the effect of any change of values: For example, a fall from 8% to 7% adds but 14% to the value of the property, while a fall from 5% to 4% adds 25% to the value of the property. Moreover, as large interest rates apply to the largest properties all further fractional lowering of low interest rates results in an enormous mass of values. The marked difference between capitalization rates of high-class and low-class property in the same city indicates the large number of people who desire to own high-class property, and the

Example of financial history of real estate. Land 89 feet by 99 feet on south corner of 16th and Laurence Streets, Denver, bought on tax title many years ago for $500. Leased 1890 for $14,000 ground rent net per annum for 99 years, or 5% on $280,000 = $3,150 per front foot. Nine-story and basement slow-burning building erected 1890, costing $325,000. Gross rents 1894, $35,200; net rents about $17,500, less ground rent $14,000, leaves $3,500, or 1% net on cost of building. Leasehold mortgaged for about $75,000; rents dropped, building surrendered to mortgagee and then to groundowner, who acquired thus a property now renting well and worth—land and building—about $300,000 (not $600,000, as at one time estimated), for an original outlay of $500.

few who desire to own low-class property. The reason for such preference is that. with high-class property, rents are more stable and easily collected, the property is more quickly and certainly convertible, it can be mortgaged at a lower rate of interest and for a larger percentage of value, the buildings depreciate much less rapidly and the prospects of increase in value are better.

That land, even of the highest type and in the largest cities, is a slow asset is due to a number of causes, among them being the fact that land is not easily passed from hand to hand as are stocks and bonds, land involves personal or directly deputed management, where stocks and bonds do not, there is no Exchange with daily quotations giving the values of land, as with stocks and bonds; and finally the value of land is influenced by many complex changing factors, whose effects are differently estimated by different people. Because land is a slow asset, convertibility, or certainty and speed in selling it, produces a high premium for the best property by lowering its capitalization rate.

CHAPTER X.

Scale of Average Values

Starting from the condition of no value in land when a city originates, let us consider the scale of average values of residence and business land in cities of various sizes, land used for other purposes being omitted as being more of an individual problem.

At the outer circumference of cities land is held as acreage, the prices per acre advancing from the normal value of farm land near cities, $50 to $150 per acre, up to market garden land, which may earn interest on $300 to $1,000 per acre, and, finally, to speculative tracts held at $500 to $5,000 per acre, whose prices are based on the estimated earnings of the land when it secures the anticipated utilization. Since the proportion of land occupied by streets averages about 35%, the conversion of acreage into lots means a loss in building area of that percentage, so that with the expenses of platting, opening streets, taxes, loss of interest, etc., it is generally estimated that property bought by the acre must sell by the lot for double the acre price in order to avoid loss in handling.

The cheapest lots in any city are those utilized for workmen's houses, varying in smaller cities from $150 to $300. The larger the city the larger the number of well-paid mechanics and the greater the effective demand for lots. A mechanic's lot on the outskirts of a small city differs from one on the outskirts of New York not only in price but in size, those in small towns having 50 to 60 feet frontage, and those in New York 15 to 20 feet frontage with usually two-family houses on them. Thus an average price of $150 for 50x100 foot lots in small cities would be equivalent to $1,300 per net acre after platting, or $850 per acre as acreage, and a price of $300 for 15x100 foot lots in large cities would be equivalent to $7,700 per net acre after platting, or $5,000 per acre as acreage. In the outskirts of the smaller cities platted land runs as low as $2 to $4 per front foot, and there are built up mechanics' sections with street car accommodation less than a mile from the centre of cities of 30,000

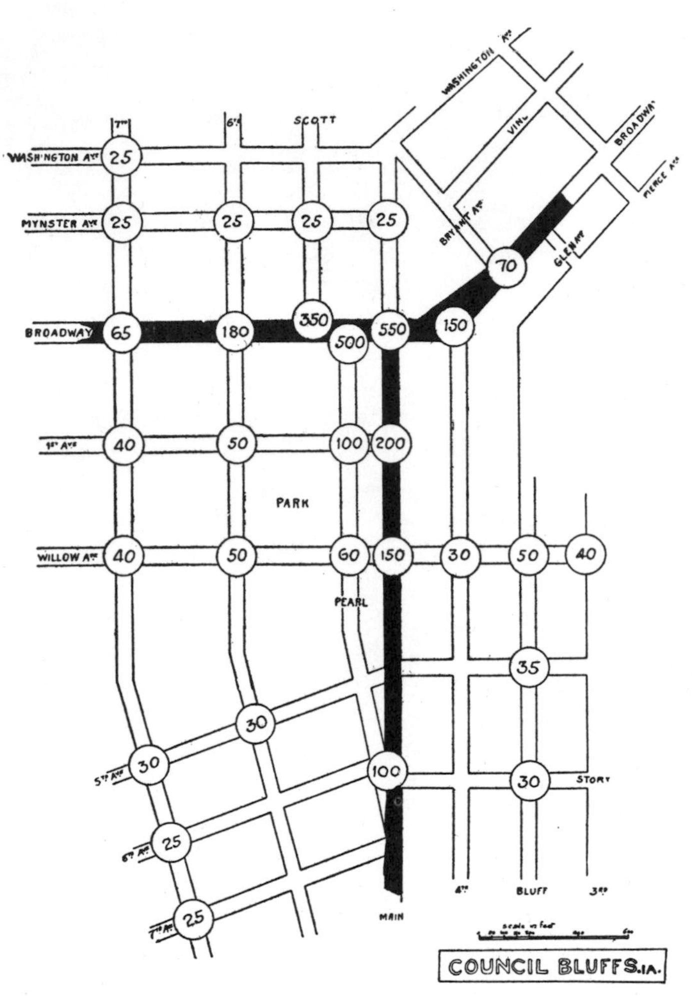

Council Bluffs. Business section. Figures represent value of corners. for lot of average width and depth, in dollars per front foot.

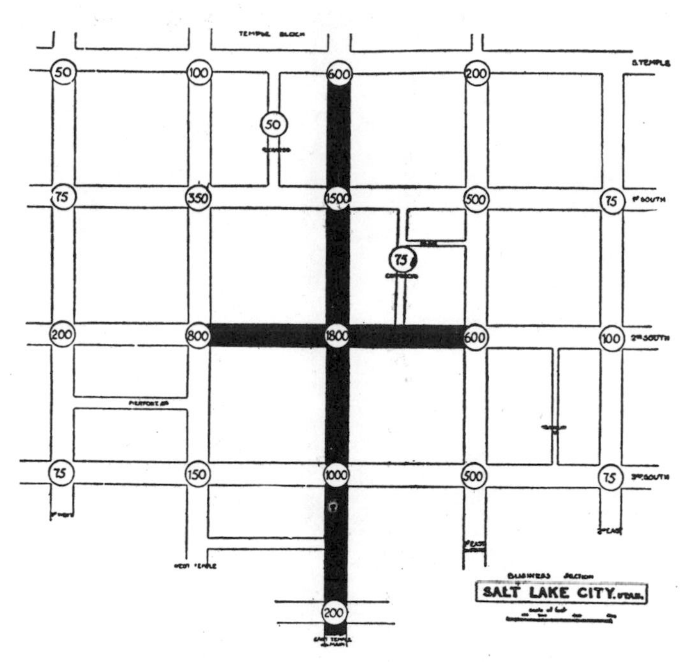

Salt Lake City. Business section. Figures represent value of corners, for lot of average width and depth, in dollars per front foot.

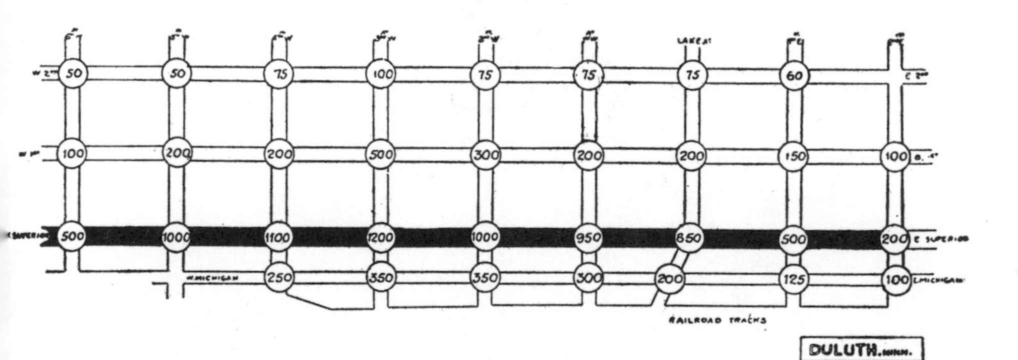

Duluth. Business section. Figures represent value of corners, for lot of average width and depth, in dollars per front foot.

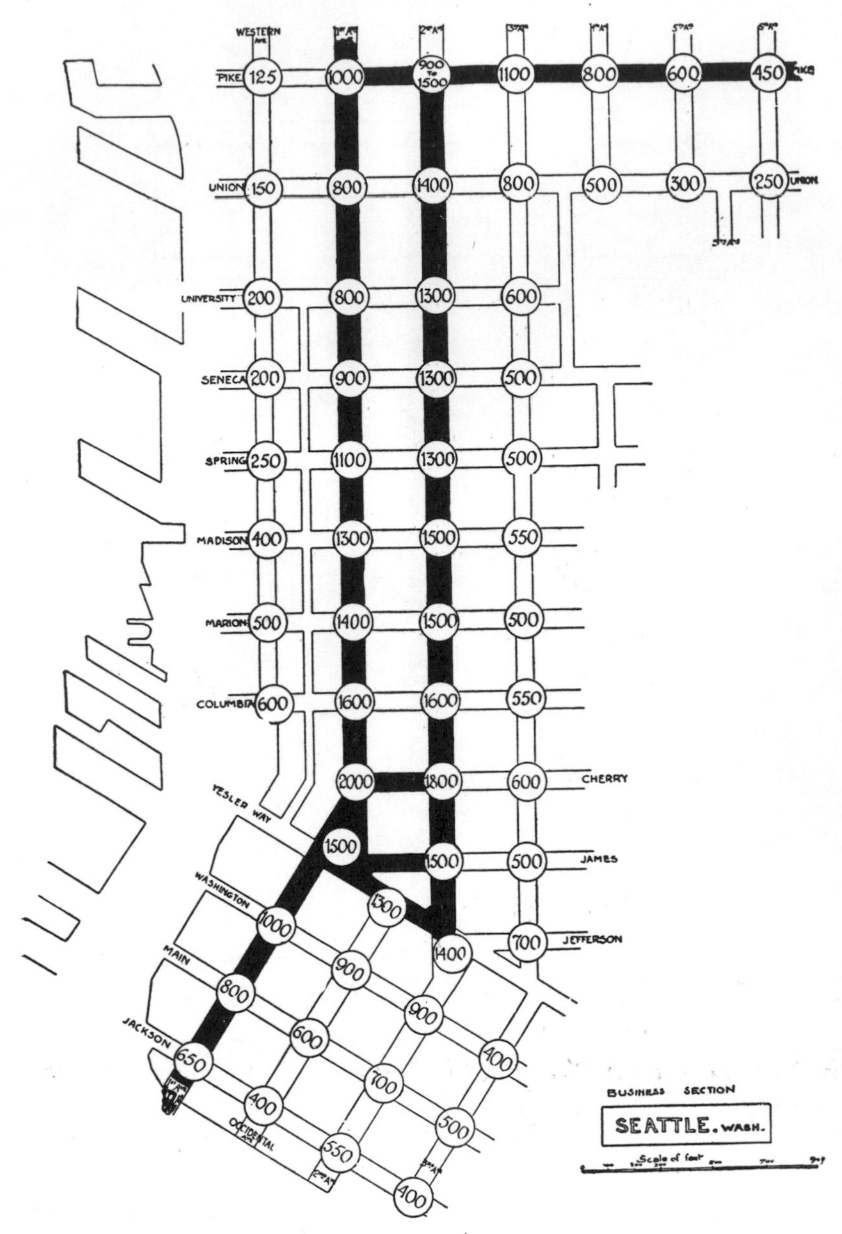

Seattle, Wash Business section, Figures represent value of corners, for lot of average width and depth, in dollars per front foot.

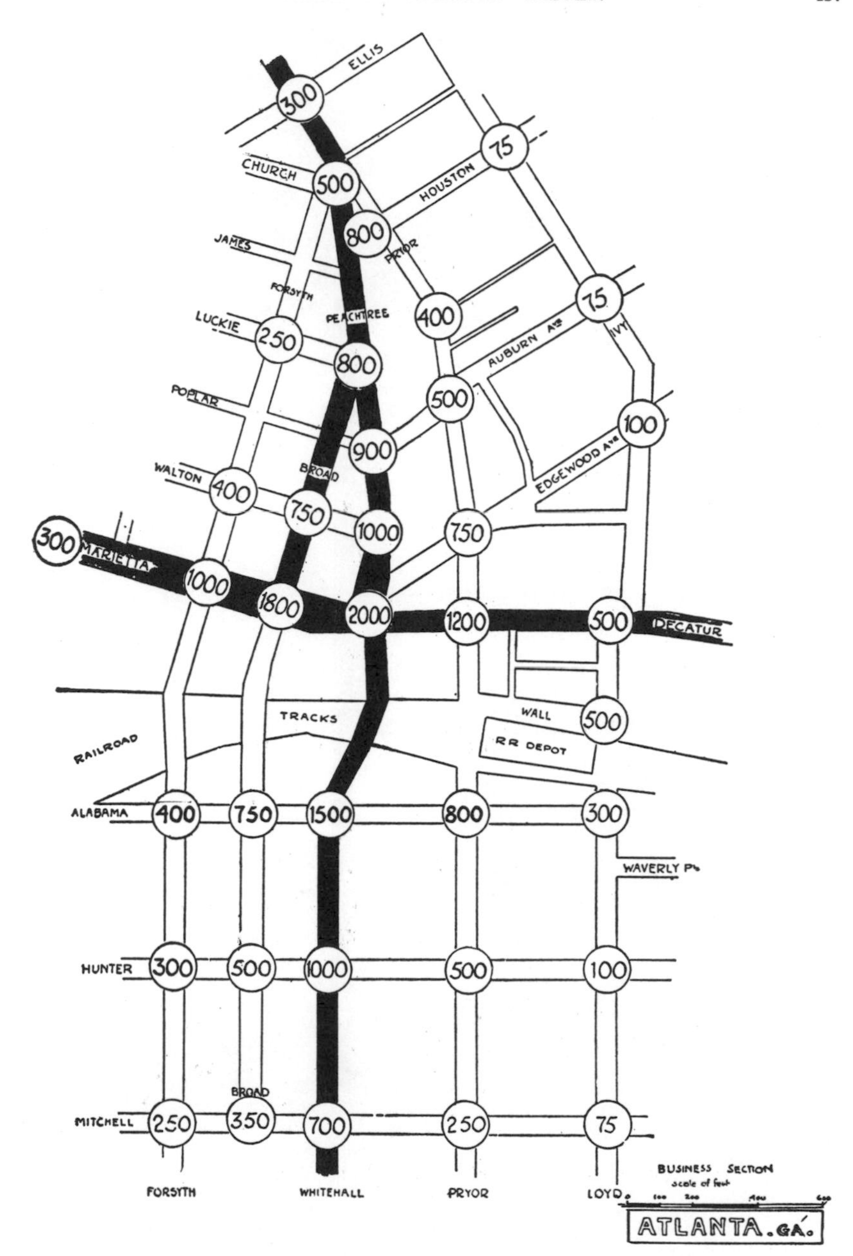

Atlanta, Ga. Business section. Figures represent value of corners, for lot of average width and depth, in dollars per front foot.

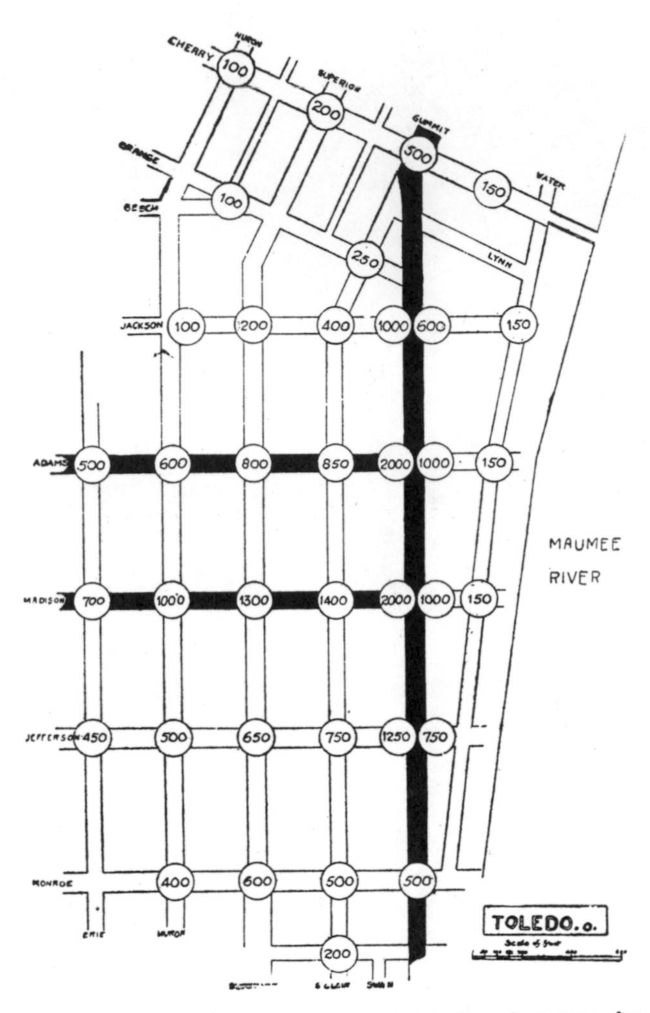

Toledo. Business section. Figures represent value of corners, for lot of average width and depth, in dollars per front foot.

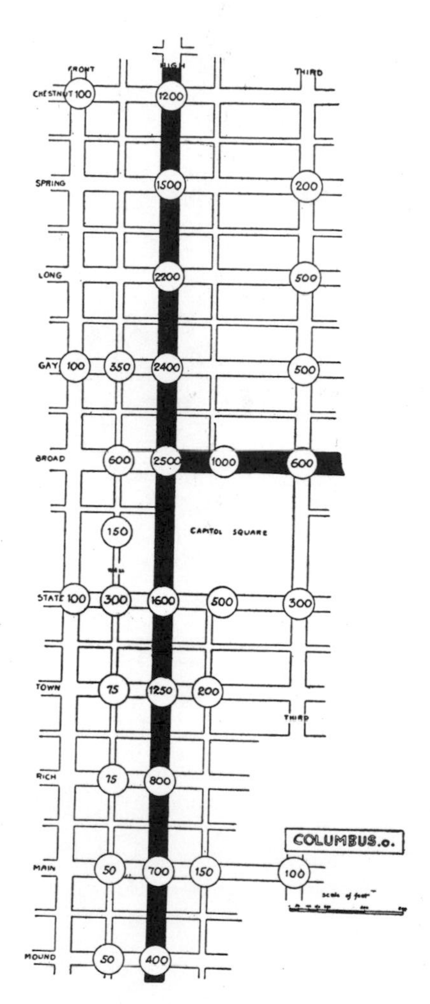

Columbus. Business section. Figures represent value of corners for lot of average width and depth, in dollars per front foot.

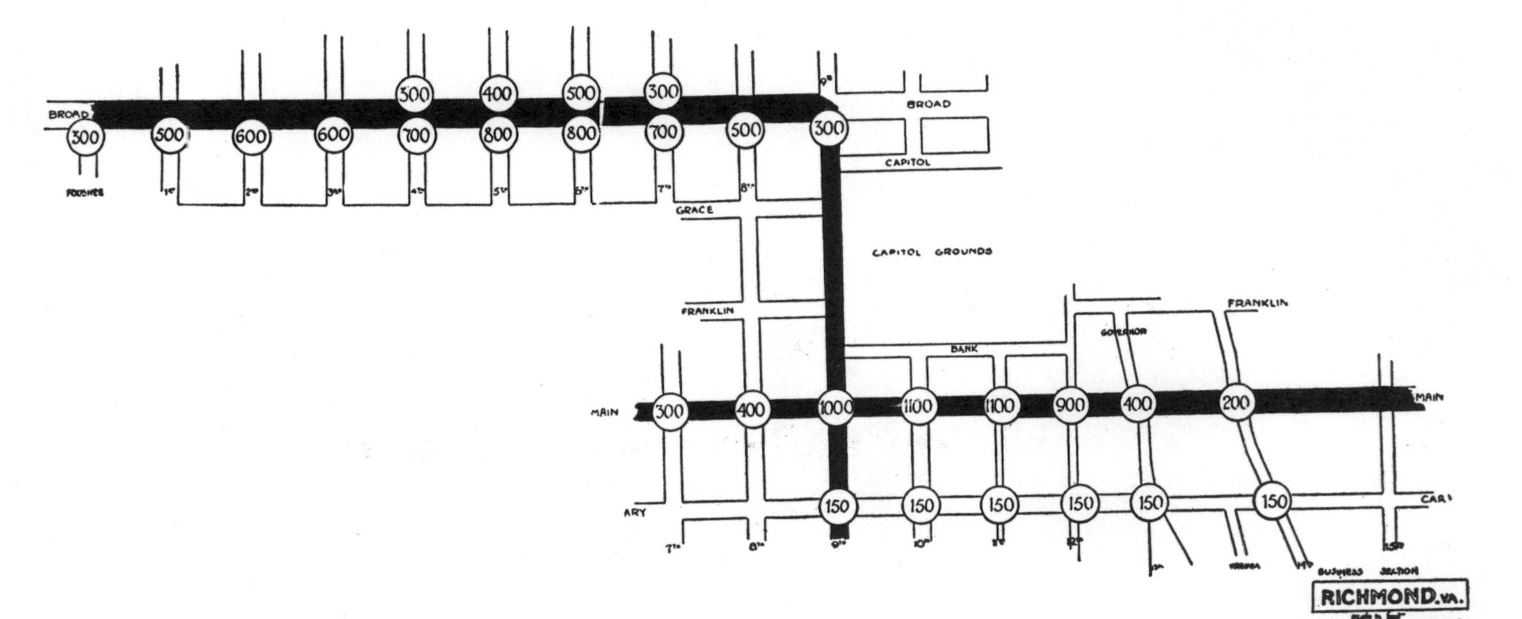

Richmond. Business section. Figures represent value of corners, for lot of average width and depth, in dollars per front foot.

population, where land sells at but $5 per front foot, equivalent to 5 cents per square foot.

From this figure, land for detached residences grades upwards more in proportion to the class of people utilizing it than the size of the city, to land worth $20 to $30 per front foot for the residences

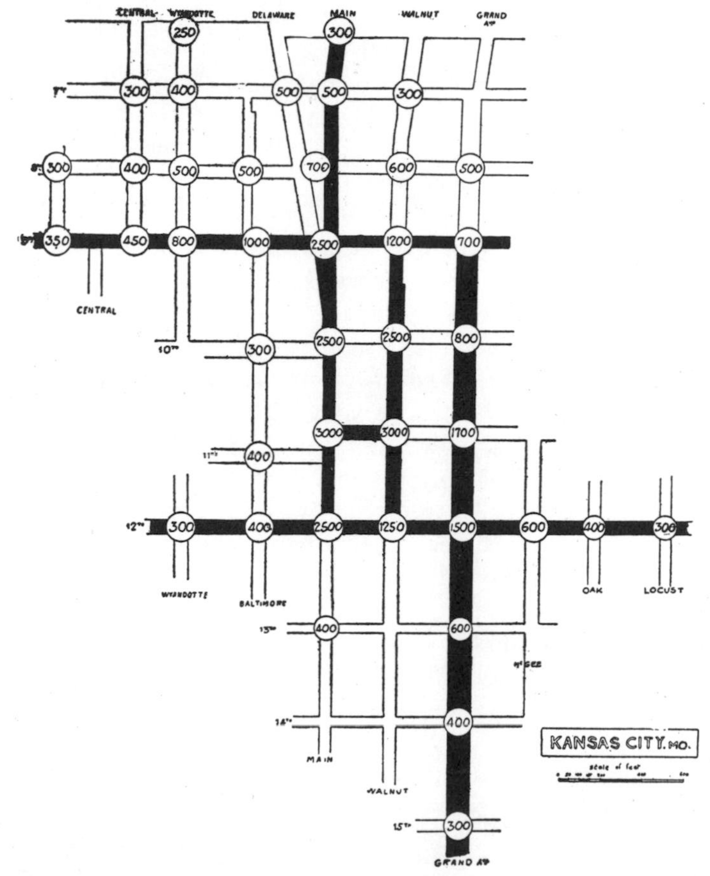

Kansas City. Business section. Figures represent value of corners for lot of average width and depth, in dollars per front foot.

of small shopkeepers and clerks, and $40 to $75 for the more fashionable residences in cities of 75,000 population and under. Such residence property would have good street car service, graded streets, sidewalks, sewer, gas, water, electric light, etc., the cost of which may vary from $5 to $15 per front foot.

The best residence land in cities of 100,000 to 200,000 population runs from $75 to $150 per front foot, in cities of 200,000 population to 400,000 population from $300 to $500 per front foot, and in New York from $2,000 to $5,000 per front foot on the side streets and $6,000 to $9,000 per front foot on Fifth Avenue.

The poorest locations utilized for shops in the small cities are ordinarily worth from $50 to $75 per front foot, from which point values rise to an average of $600 to $800 per front foot for the best business property in cities of 50,000 population, about $2,000 per front foot in cities of 200,000 population, $10,000 in cities of 2,000,000 population, and $15,000 to $18,000 in New York. Above these levels, land in the financial district of New York averages from $15,000 to $25,000 per front foot, this financial district having no counterpart in any other American city and being due to the supremacy of New York as a financial centre. The highest values in London are similarly in the financial district, while in Chicago and most of the smaller cities, shopping land, owing to the large amount of retail business and small amount of banking, is worth about twice as much as financial land. The average figures given represent corner lots having not less than 2,500 square feet, $350 per square foot (equal to $35,000 per front foot) having been paid thirty years ago for two small corners at Wall and Board Streets, and recently for a small corner at Broadway and 34th Street. An approximate scale of normal values based on the consideration that each thousand of population adds from $10 to $12 to the front foot value of the best business locations and from $1 to $2 to the front foot value of the best residence locations would be as follows, it being understood that the application of any such scale is limited in practice by differences in wealth, character of industries and inhabitants, topography, transportation, platting, climate, etc.:

TABLE I.

City population	Best business, per front ft.	Best residences, per front ft.
25,000	$300 to $400	$25 to $40
50,000	600 " 1,000	40 " 75
100,000	1,200 " 2,000	75 " 150
150,000	1,500 " 2,500	100 " 200
200,000	1,800 " 3,000	100 " 300
300,000	2,500 " 4,500	200 " 500
600,000	4,000 " 7,000	500 " 1,000
1,000,000	7,000 " 10,000	700 " 1,500
2,000,000	9,000 " 16,000	1,000 " 2,000
3,500,000	18,000 " 35,000	4,000 " 9,000

The proportion between land values due to different utilities varies widely in different cities, evidencing the response of special sections to special forces. Thus the best business and the best residence land in the same city shows in New York, with $35,000 per front foot for

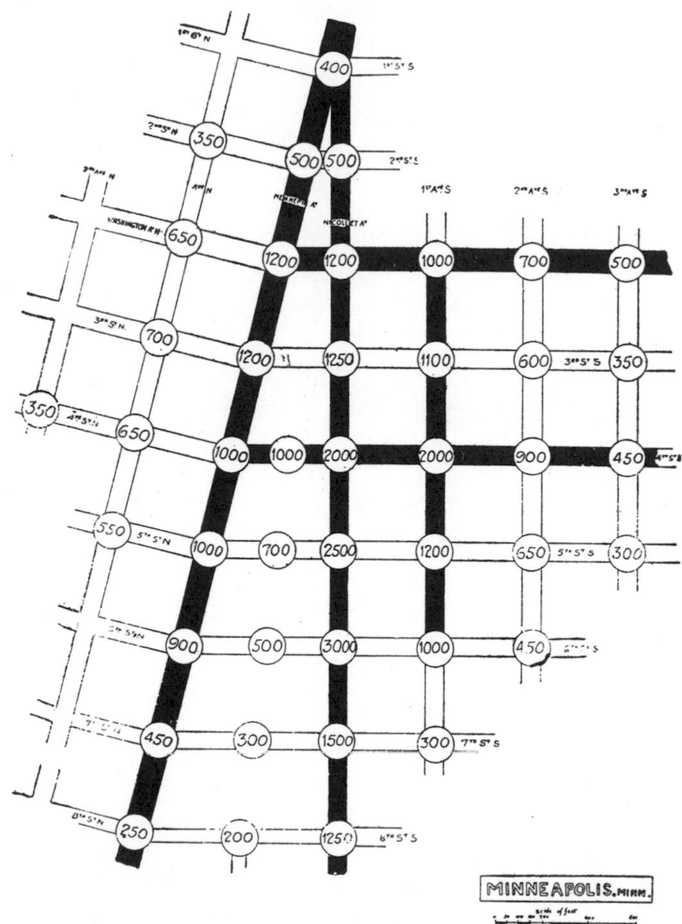

Minneapolis. Business section. Figures represent value of corners, for lot of average width and depth, in dollars per front foot.

business and $9,000 per front for residence land, a proportion of about 4 to 1; in Buffalo, with $4,500 for business land and $500 for residence land a proportion of 9 to 1; in Minneapolis, with $2,500 for business and $100 for residence land a proportion of 25 to 1; and in Seattle, with $2,500 for business and $100 for residence, a proportion of 20 to 1. When we turn to southern cities, Richmond, with $1,600 for business and $300 for residence shows a proportion of 5 to 1, and Atlanta, with $2,000 for the best business and $200 for the best residence, a proportion of 10 to 1.

As explaining this difference between western and southern cities, business is active and progressive in western cities, producing high business values, while residences are scattered by the trolley and are not held together by the old-established residence sections, whereas in southern cities the scale of business operations is less, partly owing to the diminished purchasing power of the negroes, resulting in low business values, while residence values are raised by the greater importance attached to social considerations and the greater age of the cities. The abnormally high values of residence property in New York testifies to its limited quantity and to the keen demand for it on the part of the many millionaires who make New York their home.

Heavy wholesale property responds but feebly to increased population, varying from $100 to $400 in value in cities of 300,000 people or under. Where values run above these figures the property would include some retail feature. The proportion of value between the best retail land and the best wholesale is, therefore, one which increases with the size of the city, ranging from 4 to 1 in the smaller cities, up to 10 to 1 in the largest. As examples of the value of the best retail, best wholesale and best residence land in various cities, the following list of front foot values is submitted:

TABLE II.

	Population.	Best retail.	Best wholesale.	Best residence.
New York	3,437,202	$18,000	$3,000	$9,000
Financial land	....	35,000	....	....
Chicago	1,698,575	15,000	2,000	2,000
Financial land	....	8,000	....	....
Philadelphia	1,293,697	11,000	....	2,000
Washington	278,718	5,000	....	500
Louisville	204,731	1,700	400	150
Minneapolis	202,718	2,500	400	100
Indianapolis	169,164	2,500	400	150
Kansas City	163,752	2,500	450	150
St. Paul	163,065	1,800	400	150
Denver	133,859	1,800	250	100
Toledo	131,822	2,000	300	150
Memphis	102,320	2,000	400	60
Portland, Ore.	90,426	1,600	300	70
Atlanta	89,872	2,000	400	200
Richmond	85,050	1,800	150	200
Seattle	80,671	2,000	400	80
Des Moines	62,139	1,500	200	75
Salt Lake City	53,531	1,400	200	75
Duluth	52,969	1,000	300	65
Spokane	36,848	800	200	60

CHAPTER XI.

Summary.

In reviewing the evolution of value in urban land, the first step is to conceive of the naked site apart from the buildings, having only the qualities of location and extension and without value until there is competition for land. Intrinsic value is the capitalization of the economic or ground rent, provided the buildings are suitable to the location. Exchange value consists of intrinsic value modified by future prospects. Ground rent is the residuum after deducting from gross rents all operating charges, taxes, insurance, repairs, rent collecting, and interest on the capital invested in the building. Ground rent is a premium paid solely for location and all rents are based on utility. Utilities in cities tend constantly toward specialization and complexity, business being broadly divided into distribution, administration and production, and then indefinitely subdivided; and residences being divided into as many classes as there are social grades.

In so far as land is suitable for a single purpose only, its value is proportionate to the degree to which it serves that purpose and the amount which such utility can afford to pay for it. When land is suitable for a number of purposes, one utility competes against another and the land goes to the highest utilization.

The total value of a city's site is broadly based on population and wealth, the physical city being the reflex of the total social activities of its inhabitants. Whatever the type of city, growth consists of movement away from the point of origin and is of two kinds; central, or in all directions, and axial, or along the watercourses, railroads and turnpikes which form the framework of cities. Modern rapid transit stimulates axial growth, producing star-shaped cities, whose modification in shape comes chiefly from topographical faults.

The factors distributing values over the city's area by attracting or repulsing various utilities, are, in the case of residences, absence of nuisances, good approach, favorable transportation facilities, moderate elevation and parks; in the case of retail shops, passing street traffic, with a tendency towards proximity to their customers' residences; in the case of retail wholesalers and light manufacturing, proximity to the retail stores which are their customers; in the case of heavy wholesaling or manufacturing, proximity to transportation; and in the case of public or semi-public buildings, for historical reasons, proximity to the old business centre; the land that is finally left being filled in with mingled cheap utilities, parasites of the stronger utilities, which give a low earning power to land otherwise valueless.

Value by proximity responds to central growth, diminishing in

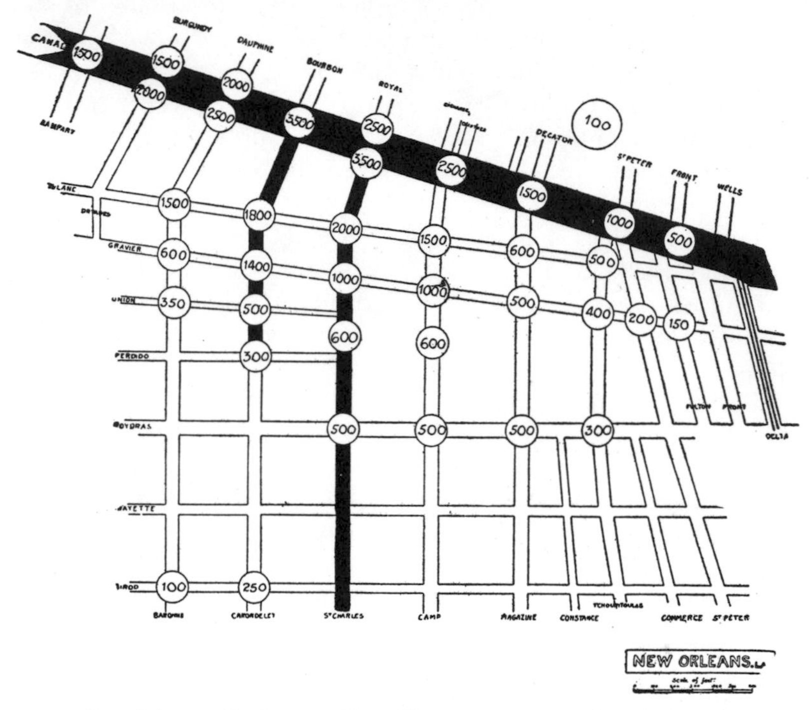

New Orleans. Business section. Figures represent value of corners, for lot of average width and depth, in dollars per front foot.

proportion to distance from various centres, while value from accessibility responds to axial growth, diminishing in proportion to absence of transportation facilities. Change occurs not only at the circumference but throughout the whole area of a city, outward growth being due both to pressure from the centre and to aggregation at the edges. All buildings within a city react upon each other, superior and inferior utilities displacing each other in turn. Whatever the size or shape of a city and however great the complexity of its

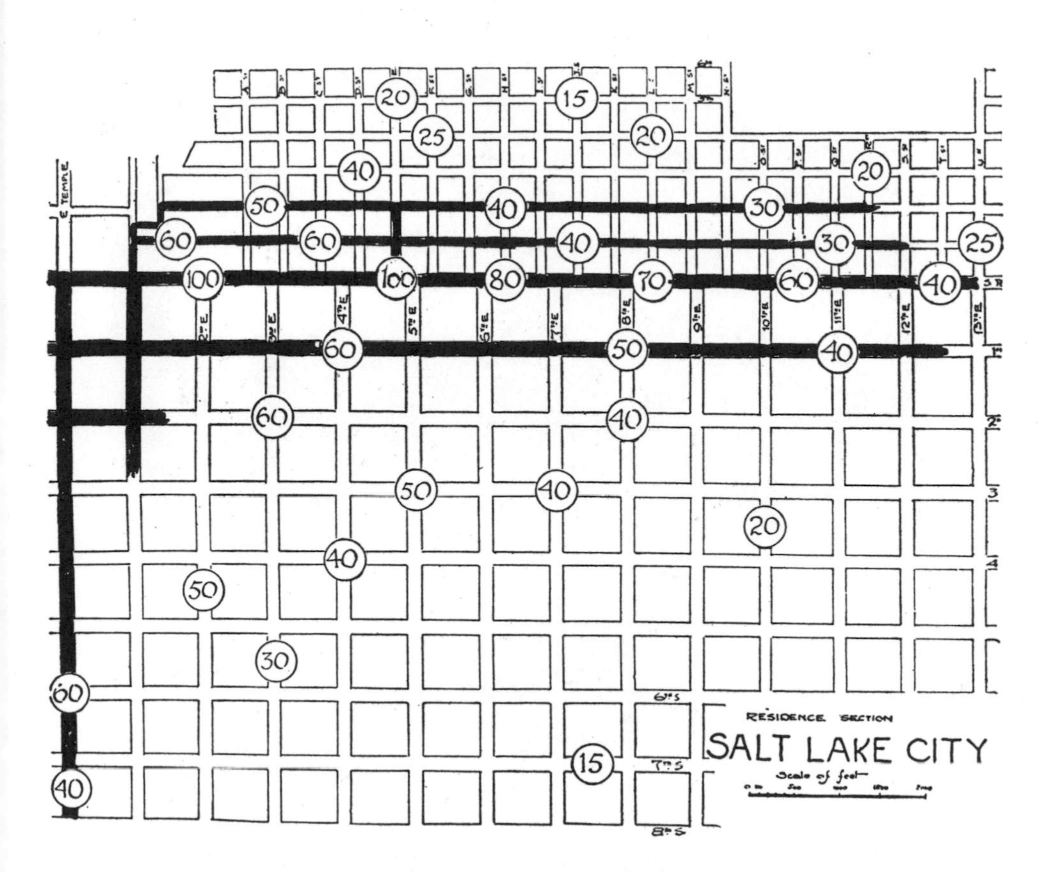

Salt Lake City. Residence section. Figures represent value of corners, for lot of average width and depth, in dollars per front foot.

utilities, the order of dependence of one upon another is based on simple principles, all residences seeking attractive surroundings and all business seeking its customers.

While the outward glacial movement of a city continues, the daily currents of travel within alter its internal structure. The fluidity of daily traffic shifts utilities, creates plastic conditions in cities and keeps values in a state of unstable equilibrium.

To look at the problem from the individual standpoint, in attempt-

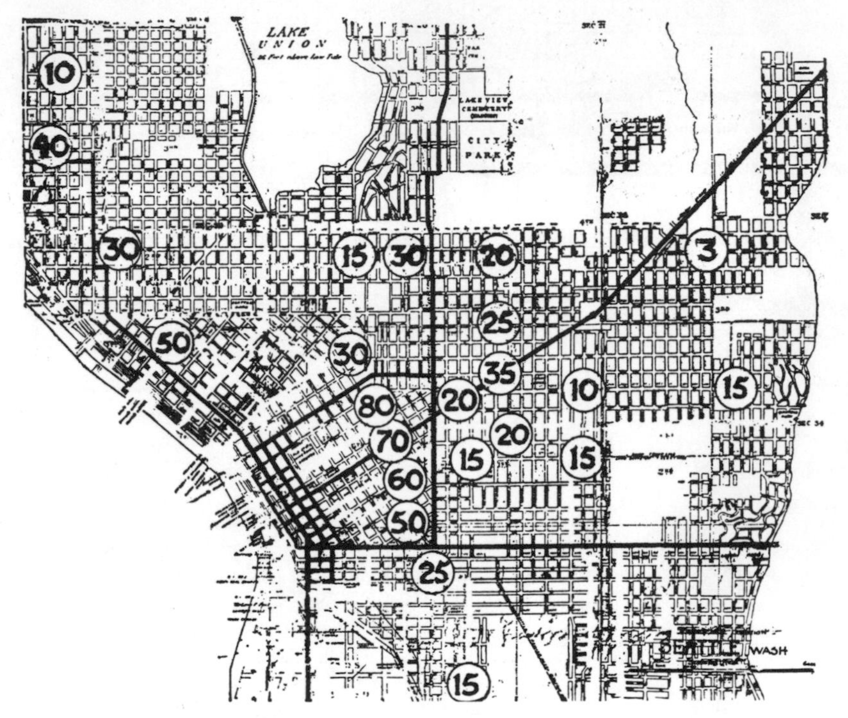

Seattle. Residence section. Figures represent value of corners, for lot of average width and depth, in dollars, per front foot.

ing to state the value of any single property, the inquiry would seek first, upon what forces does the city itself depend, how permanent are they, how diversified, are they strengthening and what is the resulting index figure, to wit, the rate of increase of the city's population; next, what are the characteristics of the section of the city in which the property is located, its past history, its present stability, its future prospects; what is the central strength of the property, how near the main centre of the city or the various sub-centers of attraction; what is its axial strength, the quantity, quality and regularity of the passing travel, what is the character of building on the property as to suitability, planning, physical condition, prospect of changing utility, management, convertibility, gross and net income; at what prices have surrounding property been selling, are they rising or falling, and do they suggest any factors not yet taken into account; is the property liable to be injured or benefited by changes in the building laws; is there any special enterprise or strength on the part

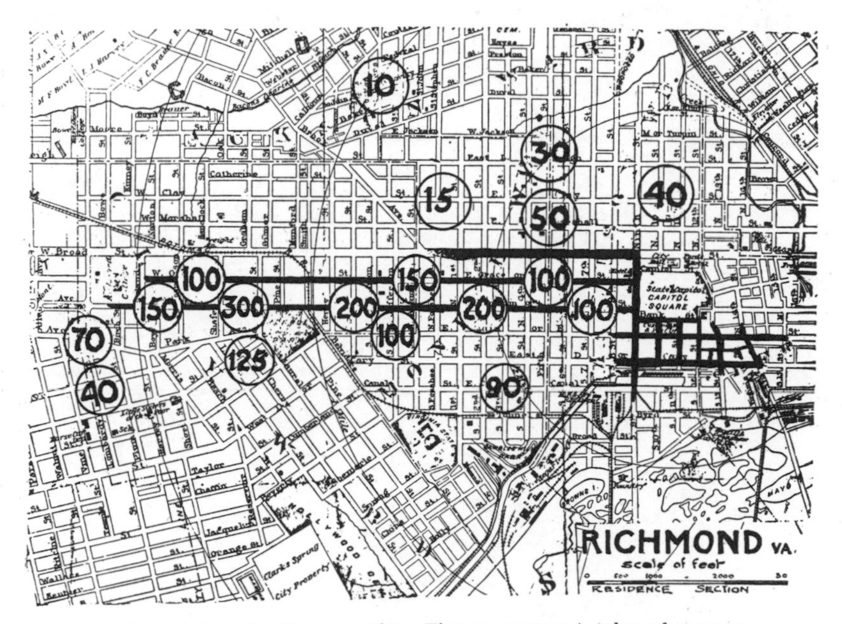

Richmond, Va. Residence section. Figures represent value of corners, for lot of average width and depth, in dollars per front foot.

of the owner or of surrounding district likely to affect the property, what would be the probable effect of any inventions or improvements in transportation or the construction of buildings, and, finally, what are the general commercial conditions as affecting the earning power of tenants, actual or prospective, and financial conditions as affecting the capitalization rate.

The problem is never a simple one, being as complex as city life itself, but it is not insoluble, since the forces creating cities are governed by uniform laws, like causes producing like results, apparent exceptions being due to the influence of factors not reckoned on. The popular impression that the ability to forecast future movements

Columbus, O. Residence section. Figures represent value of corners, for lot of average width and depth, in dollars per front foot.

Atlanta. Residence section. Figures represent value of corners, for lot of average width and depth, in dollars per front foot.

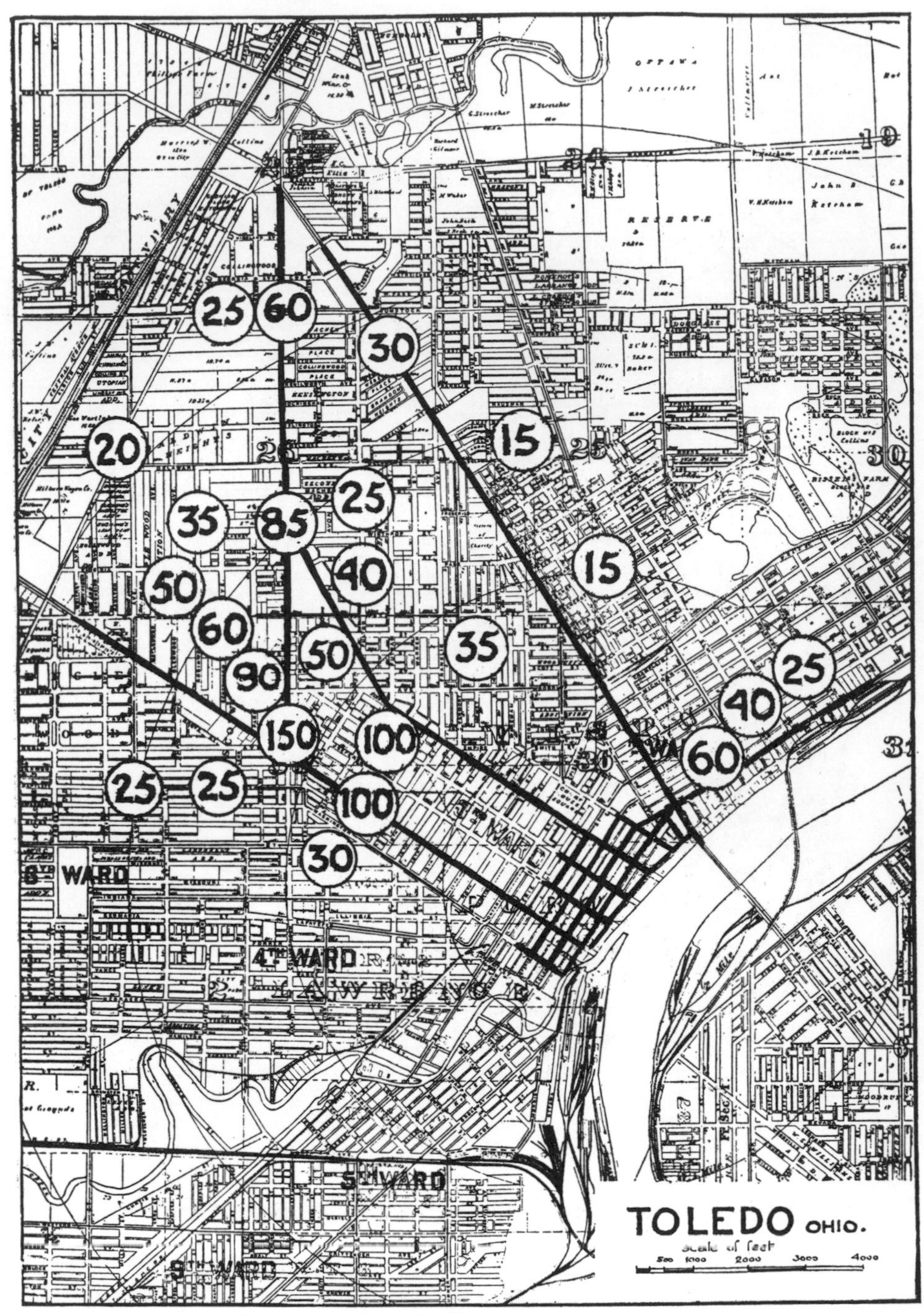

Toledo. Residence section. Figures represent value of corners, for lot of average width and depth, in dollars per front foot.

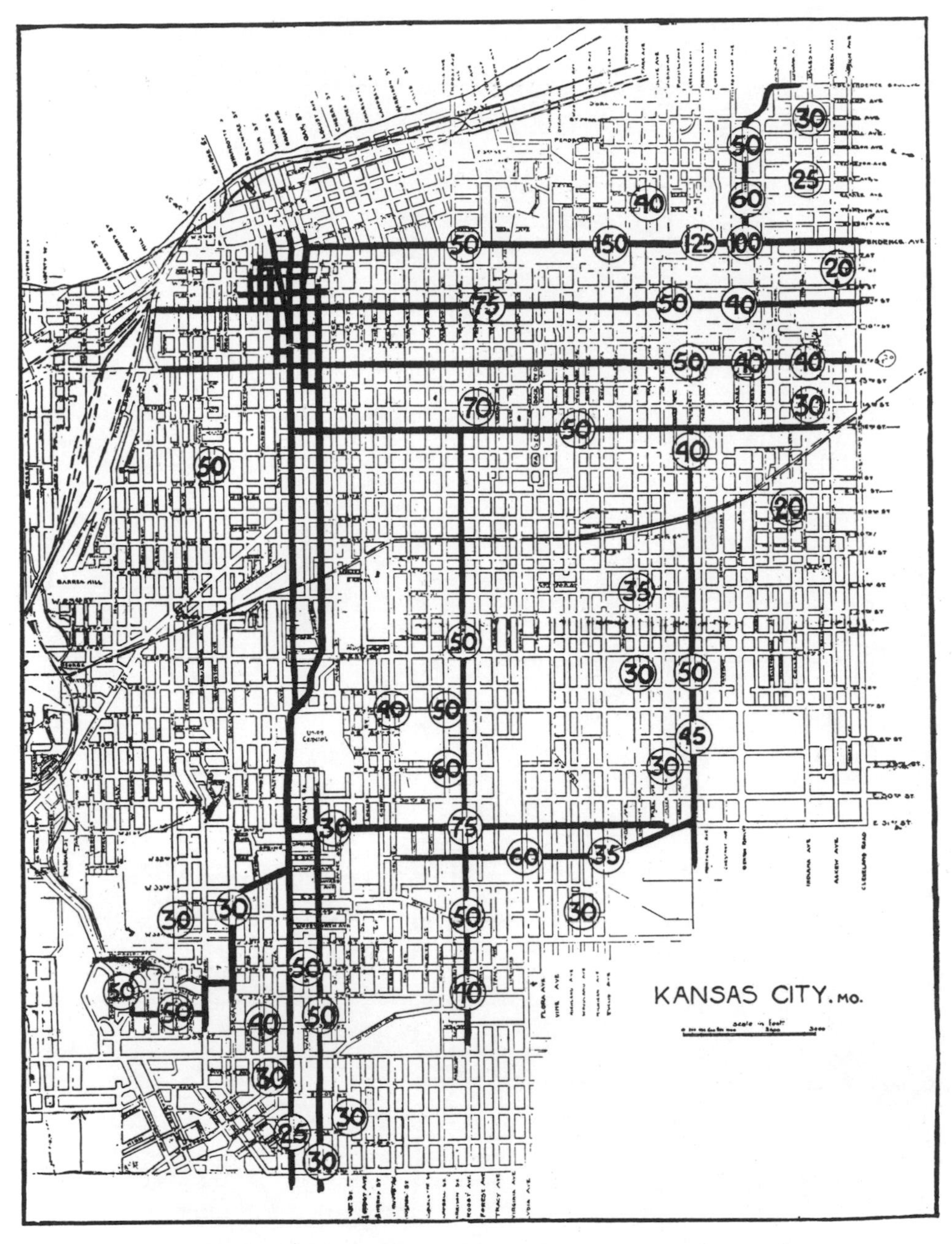

Kansas City, Mo. Residence section. Figures represent value of corners, for lot of average width and depth, in dollars per front foot.

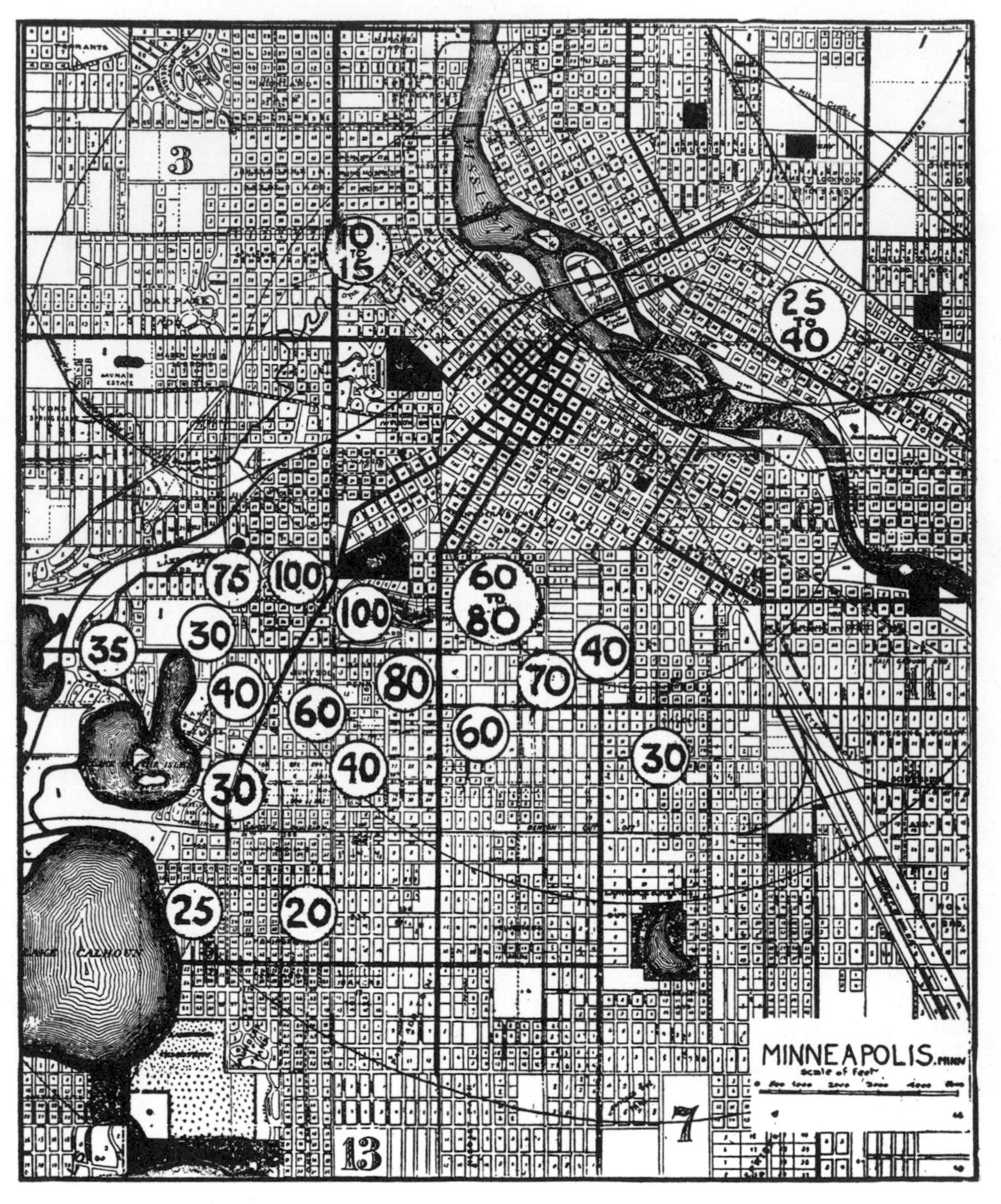

Minneapolis. Residence sections. Figures represent value of corners. for lot of average width and depth, in dollars per front foot.

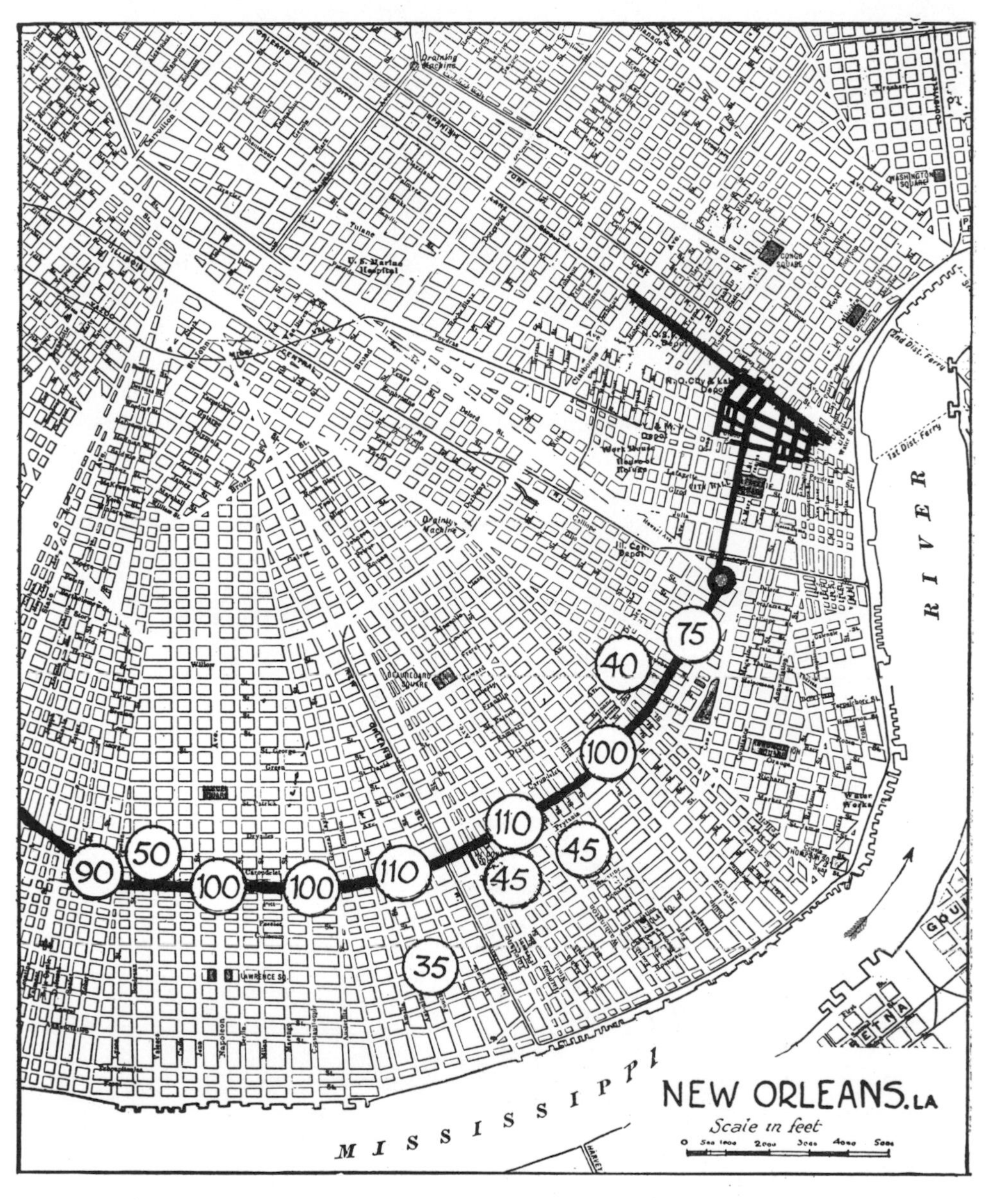

New Orleans. Residence section in American quarter. Figures represent value of corners, for lot of average width and depth, in dollars per front foot.

of city growth points a quick way to fortune is an over estimate, since real estate movements are slow, large capital is required to handle it, carrying charges are heavy, and even though the forecast may be ultimately correct, the rate of movement is uncertain, depending on the operation of vast economic forces impossible of exact prediction.

If business expands and population increases in a city, the sum total of land vlaues is certain to increase. All the land, however, will by no means increase in value, the great mass of medium business and residence property advancing but slowly since it supplies the wants of a large number of people of moderate earning power who cannot pay beyond a certain price. Coincident with the gradual lifting of values as population becomes more dense, decaying sections, left behind in the onward march, drop down the scale of inferior utilities and values, sometimes to the point of extinction. Such worn-out property exhibits in its dilapidations both absence of utility and public confession of that fact. If population and business become stationary the sum total of land values will decrease in proportion to the previous discounting of future growth, subsequent movements consisting of redistribution of value, as one part of the city or another, or one individual or another, flourishes or declines.

The principal causes of the redistribution of value in all cities are, increase in population and wealth, especially in causing relocation or extension of the best residence district, changes in transportation, such as new surface, elevated, or underground lines, new bridges, tunnels, ferries and railroads, and the readjustments of new utilities in new areas harmonizing the complex contending factors.

Present tendencies point towards greatly increased values at strategic points, with relative and frequently absolute drops in value in locations formerly competitive. The quiet side streets, the back alleys and deserted nooks and corners where land has almost no value, despite its proximity to valuable land, will doubtless continue at their present low planes, unless they are either reached by the spreading growth from some center or are intersected by some new traffic street.

The point of highest value, responding in scale and location to the growth of the city, moves from the first business centre towards the best residence district, the crest of the wave being usually the middle of the retail shopping district, frequently strengthened by exceptionally large and handsome buildings, and occasionally checked by cross traffic streets. Apart from any factors which may deflect

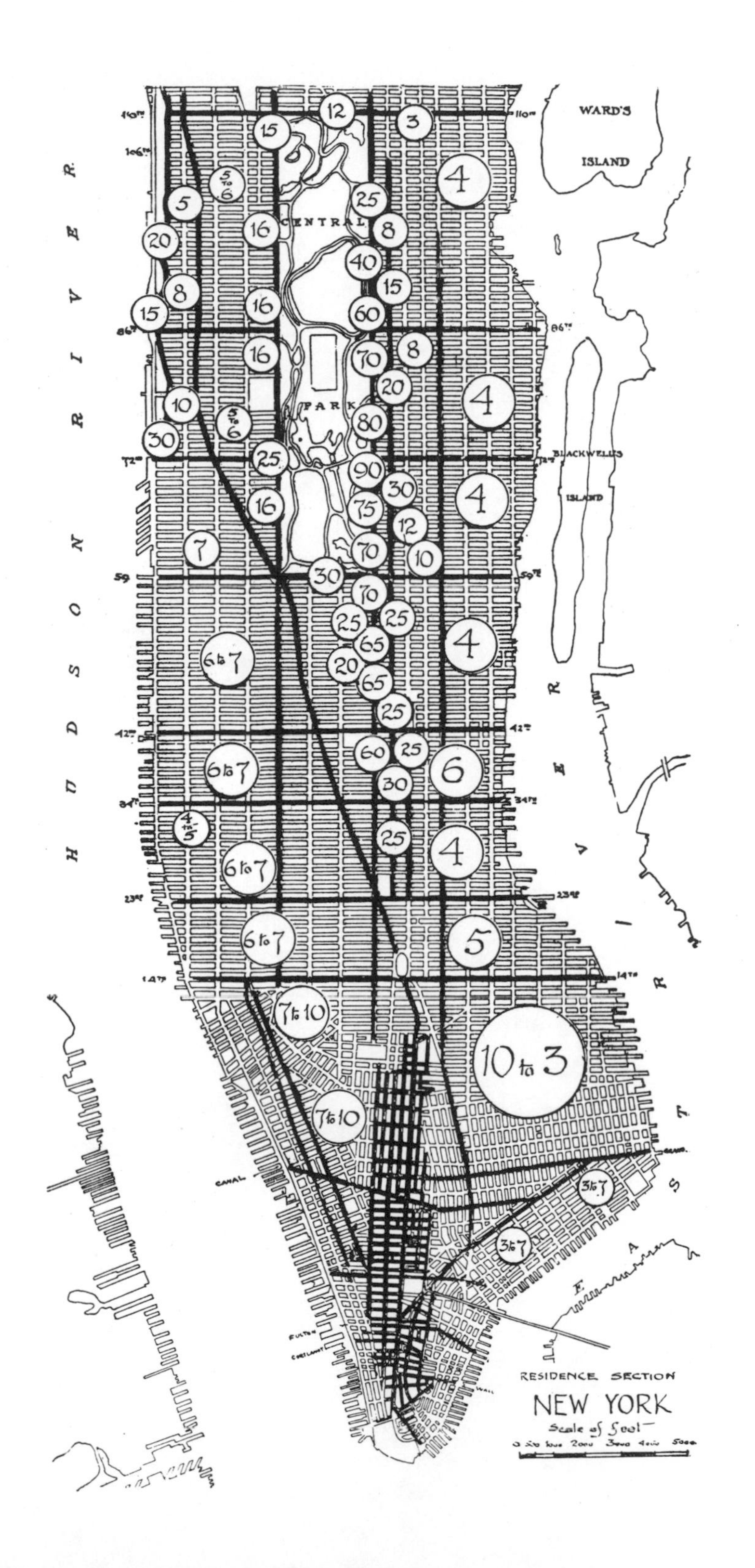
HUDSON RIVER
EAST RIVER
WARD'S ISLAND
BLACKWELLS ISLAND
CENTRAL PARK
110th
106th
86th
72nd
59th
42nd
34th
23rd
14th
CANAL
FULTON
CORTLANDT
WALL
RESIDENCE SECTION
NEW YORK
Scale of Feet
0 500 1000 2000 3000 4000 5000

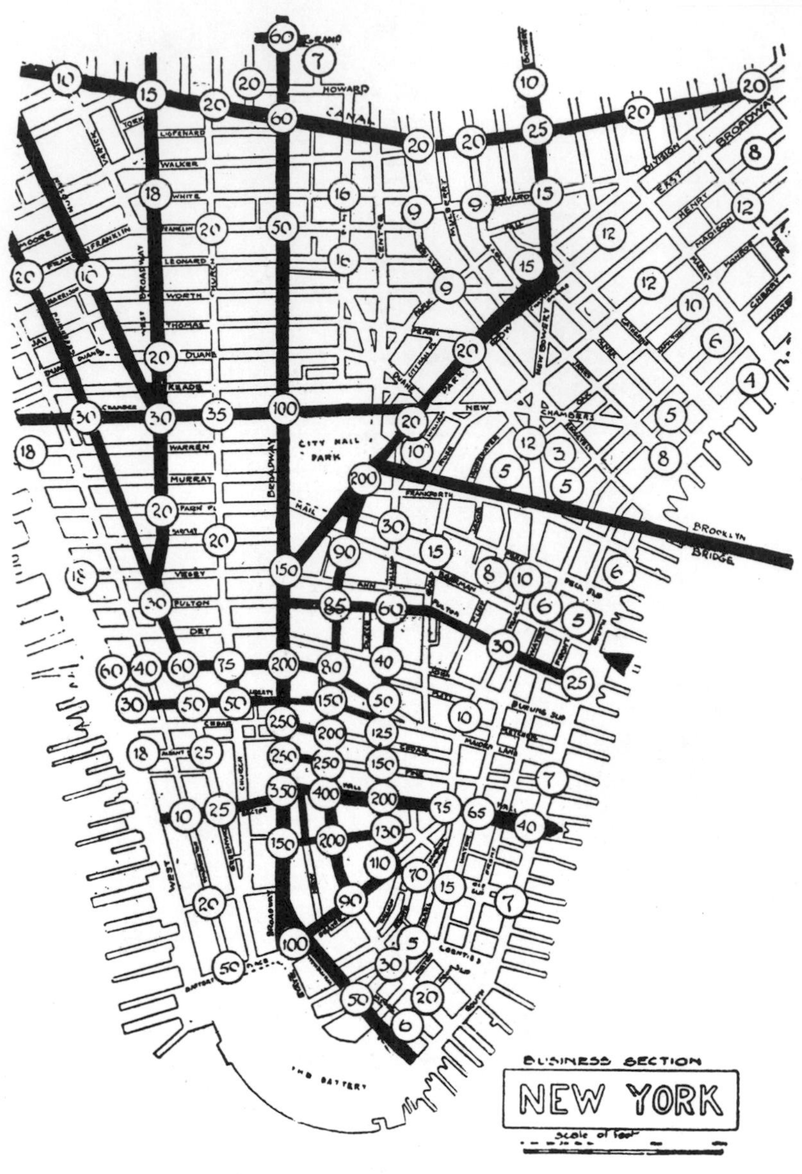

Map Showing Value per Square Foot in Dollars of New York Real Estate.-

the line of growth, the land lying in its path is certain to increase in value, the time of such increase, however, being difficult to gauge, while the land left behind will usually sink in value, although in the largest cities, while decreasing relatively in value and utility, it sometimes increases slightly in absolute value. New York, the one financial centre of the country, is an exception in that its financial land is more valuable than its shopping land.

New inventions and new habits and customs will probably cause the most marked future changes other than those due to growth or transportation. All cheapening of the cost of buildings, all improvements in construction, all inventions, tend constantly to destroy the value of existing buildings. All improvements in transportation, such as the trolley, the elevated, the underground, the bicycle, the automobile—and in future possibly the flying machine—tend to destroy the value of these locations which depend on existing transportation. All changes in social customs, such as longer summer absences from the city, shift values, as in this instance from the city to the summer resorts. The great interchange of travel throughout the year from one city to another strengthens the radiating influence of the hotels, while the movement from residences to flats and apartments, concentrates population and augments the power of capital to attract.

Change is a law of life, and as long as human activity continues to alter the conditions of city life, and human tastes, prejudices, fashions, habits and customs continue to vary, city structure and values will shift and change, but the study of the basic principles of city growth should reduce errors in forecasting to a minimum, permitting well equipped intelligence, whether in buying, selling, renting, loaning on, or in any way dealing with city real estate, to largely eliminate the power of chance.